Virginia General   Assembly Senate

Senate Bills Extra Session 1861

Virginia General   Assembly Senate

Senate Bills Extra Session 1861

ISBN/EAN: 9783337163440

Printed in Europe, USA, Canada, Australia, Japan

Cover: Foto ©Suzi / pixelio.de

More available books at **www.hansebooks.com**

BILL No. 1.

SENATE BILL.

A BILL

To provide for electing Members of a Convention, and to convene the same.

1. Be it enacted by the General Assembly, That it shall be the
2 duty of the superintendents and officers who were appointed to super-
3 intend and conduct elections for county officers in May last, at the
4 places established for holding elections for members of the General
5 Assembly, to open polls for electing delegates to a Convention, to
6 consider and propose such measures as may be expedient for this
7 Commonwealth to adopt in the present crisis of State and National
8 affairs. The said election shall be held on the   day of Feb-
9 ruary, in the year of our Lord 1861.

2. The Convention shall consist of one hundred and fifty-two
2 members, to be chosen for and by the several counties and cities of
3 the Commonwealth, as prescribed by the second section of the fourth
4 article of the Constitution of this State, for the election of members
5 of the House of Delegates. The county or counties which alter-
6 nately vote for delegates to the General Assembly, under the said
7 article of the Constitution, and which, at the next election for dele-

8 gates, would be entitled to elect a delegate or delegates, shall elect
9 the same number of members of the Convention, and in the same
10 manner that they would be entitled to, if the election were for
11 members of the next session of the General Assembly.

3. Any person may be elected a member of the Convention, who
2 at the time of election has attained the age of twenty-five years,
3 and is a citizen of this Commonwealth.

4. The said election shall, in all respects, be conducted in the
2 mode prescribed, and the officers conducting the same shall be vested
3 with the powers, perform the duties, receive the same compensation,
4 and be liable to the penalties prescribed by law for general elections,
5 except as herein prescribed.

5. The polls shall remain open for one day only, and the com-
2 missioners superintending the said election, at the courthouses, shall
3 meet in their respective counties and corporations, on the second
4 day after the election day: shall then compare the polls for their
5 respective counties and corporations which elect a delegate or dele-
6 gates, and ascertain and certify the votes of the counties and
7 corporations, or parts thereof, comprising election districts, and
8 deliver a certified statement thereof to the officers conducting the
9 election at the courthouses.

10   And, to compare the returns from the respective counties and
11 parts of counties forming election districts for members of the
12 General Assembly, the officers conducting the election at the court-
13 houses of the respective counties and parts of counties of such

14 election districts, shall meet and compare the returns at the places
15 now required by law for such comparison, on the fourth day after
16 the election, and make returns of the *election*.

6. The members so chosen, shall meet on the   day
2 of February next, and proceed to adopt such measures as they may
3 deem expedient for the welfare of the Commonwealth.   The sessions
4 of the said Convention shall be held in the capitol, until otherwise
5 provided by law.

7. In the case of a contested election, the same shall be gov-
2 erned in all respects by the existing laws in regard to contested elec-
3 tions in the House of Delegates.

8. In case of vacancies occurring previous to the meeting of the
2 Convention, the Governor shall issue writs to supply the same; and
3 after the said meeting, the writs shall be issued by order of the Con-
4 vention; and the elections under such writs shall be conducted in all
5 respects as the elections hereinbefore provided for.

9. The said Convention shall be the judge of its own privileges
2 and elections, and the members thereof shall have, possess and enjoy,
3 in the most full and ample manner, all the privileges which members
4 elected to and attending on the General Assembly are entitled to, and
5 moreover shall be allowed the same pay for traveling to, attending
6 on, and returning from the said Convention as is now allowed to
7 members of the General Assembly for like services.

10. The said Convention is hereby empowered to appoint such
2 officers, and to make them such reasonable allowances for their ser-

3 vices as it shall deem proper; which several allowances shall be
4 audited by the Auditor of Public Accounts, and paid by the Treasurer
5 of the Commonwealth, out of any money in the treasury not other-
6 wise appropriated.

11. The expenses incurred in providing poll books and in pro-
2 curing writers to keep the same, shall be defrayed as heretofore in the
3 elections of members of the General Assembly.

12. Immediately upon the passage of this act, the Governor
2 shall issue a proclamation giving notice thereof, the times of holding
3 the election, and of the meeting of the Convention herein provided
4 for.

13. The Secretary of the Commonwealth shall cause to be sent
2 to the clerks of each county and corporation as many copies of this
3 act as there are precincts therein, using for that purpose special mes-
4 sengers, when in his judgment it shall be necessary; and it shall be
5 the duty of the said clerks to deliver the same to the sheriffs of their
6 respective counties or corporations, who shall cause a copy to be
7 posted at the door of the courthouse, and at some public place in
8 each election district.

14. This act shall be in force from its passage.

SUBSTITUTE

Offered by Mr. Thomas of Henry, for Bill No. 1, to provide for electing members of a Convention, and to convene the same.

1. Be enacted by the General Assembly, That it shall be the
2 duty of the commissioners and other officers who were appointed to
3 conduct elections for county officers in May last at the places es-
4 tablished for holding elections for members of the General Assem-
5 bly, to open a separate poll for the purpose of taking the sense of
6 the people upon the question, whether they desire a Convention or
7 not. The poll to be opened, shall contain two columns; one for the
8 names of those who vote in the affirmative, the other for the names
9 of those who vote in the negative, and shall be headed thus:

10 "Shall there be a Convention to consider and propose such mea-
11 sures as may be expedient for this Commonwealth to adopt in the
12 present crisis of State and National affairs."

CONVENTION. | NO CONVENTION.

2. At the same time and places, said commissioner and other
2 officers shall open other polls for electing delegates to such Conven-
3 tion, in case such Convention shall be called by a majority of the
4 people. This poll to be taken, and elections made on the
5 day of   in the present year.

3. No person shall be permitted to vote on the question afore-
2 said, and in the election aforesaid, who is not entitled to vote for
3 delegates to the General Assembly under the existing laws of this
4 Commonwealth.

4. The Convention, if ordained by a majority of the votes thus
2 taken, shall consist of one hundred and fifty-two members, to be
3 chosen for, and by the several counties and cities of the Common-
4 wealth, as prescribed by the second section of the fourth article of
5 the Constitution of this State, for the election of members of the
6 House of Delegates. The county or counties which alternately
7 vote for delegates to the General Assembly under the said article of
8 the Constitution, and which at the next election for delegates, would
9 be entitled to elect a delegate or delegates, shall elect the same
10 number of members of the Convention, and in the same manner
11 that they would be entitled to, if the election were for members of
12 the next session of the General Assembly.

5. Any person may be elected a member of such Convention,
2 who, at the time of election has attained the age of twenty-five
3 years, and is actually a citizen of this Commonwealth.

6. The said election shall, in all respects, be conducted in the
2 mode prescribed, and the commissioners 'and other officers conduct-
3 ing the same, shall be vested with the powers, perform the duties,
4 and be liable to the penalties prescribed by the Code of Virginia for
5 general elections, except as herein provided.

7. The polls shall remain open for one day only; and the com-

2 missioners superintending the said polls, shall meet in their respec-

3 tive counties, corporations and election districts on the

4 day from the commencement of the election; shall then ascertain

5 the state of the poll on the question of "Convention" or "No Con-

6 vention," and forthwith certify the result to the Governor of the

7 Commonwealth by mail or express as said commissioners shall deem

8 best to ensure the receipt thereof within one week after said elec-

9 tion. They shall then compare the polls of election, and decide who

10 is elected, and shall make returns of the election; one of which

11 they shall forthwith transmit by mail or express to the Governor;

12 another, together with a certificate of the vote upon the question of

13 "Convention" or "No Convention," and with all the poll books,

14 shall be delivered to the clerk of the county or corporation court, to

15 be filed in his office, and another to the member or members elected

16 to said Convention.

8. Upon receiving said certificates and returns, it shall first be

2 the duty of the Governor to ascertain the result of the vote upon

3 the question of "Convention" or "No Convention," and if the result

4 be found to be in favor of the call of the Convention, the Governor

5 shall issue a proclamation, convening the members so chosen on

6   , who shall meet

7 at the capitol, in the city of Richmond accordingly, and proceed to

8 adopt such measures as they shall deem expedient for the welfare of

9 the Commonwealth; provided, however, that any act or ordinance

10 for the withdrawal of the State from the Union, or her confedera-

11 tion with any other State, shall be submitted to the voters of the
12 Commonwealth for ratification or rejection. But if the result of
13 the vote shall be found to be against the Convention, the Governor
14 shall cause the result of all the certificates made from all the coun-
15 ties and corporations respectively, within the Commonwealth, to be
16 published by proclamation.

9. In the case of a contested election, the proceedings shall be
2 governed in all respects by the existing laws in regard to contested
3 elections in the House of Delegates, and the Convention shall de-
4 cide it.

10. In case of vacancies occurring previous to the meeting of
2 the Convention, the Governor shall issue writs to supply the same;
3 and after the said meeting, the writs shall be issued by order of the
4 Convention, and the elections under such writs shall be conducted
5 in all respects as the elections hereinbefore provided for.

11. The said Convention shall be the judge of its own privileges
2 and elections, and the members thereof shall have, possess and enjoy,
3 in the most full and ample manner, all the privileges which members
4 elected to and attending on the General Assembly are entitled to,
5 and, moreover, shall be allowed the same pay for traveling to, at-
6 tending on and returning from the said Convention as is now allowed
7 to members of the General Assembly for like services.

12. The said Convention is hereby empowered to appoint such
2 officers, and to make them such reasonable allowances for their ser-

3 vices as it shall deem proper; which several allowances shall be
4 audited by the Auditor of Public Accounts, and paid by the Treas-
5 urer of the Commonwealth out of any money in the Treasury not
6 otherwise appropriated.

13. The expenses incurred in providing poll books, employing
2 writers to keep the same, or expresses to forward certificates and
3 returns with dispatch, shall be defrayed as in the election of mem-
4 bers of the General Assembly.

14. This act shall be in force from its passage.

SENATE BILL.

A BILL

Changing the Time of holding the Terms of the Circuit Courts of James City and the city of Williamsburg and the county of Henrico.

1. Be it enacted by the General Assembly, That the thirteenth
2 section of chapter one hundred and fifty-eight of the Code of Vir-
3 ginia, be altered and re-enacted so as to read as follows:

4 "§ 13. In the sixth circuit: for the county of Elizabeth City, on
5 the fifteenth day of March and fifteenth day of September; for the
6 county of Warwick, on the twenty-first day of March and twenty-
7 first day of September; for the county of York, on the twenty-sixth
8 day of March and twenty-sixth day of September; for the county
9 of Gloucester, on the thirteenth day of April and thirteenth day of
10 October; for the county of Matthews, on the sixth day of April and
11 sixth day of October; for the county of Middlesex, on the first day
12 of April and first day of October; for the county of James City and
13 city of Williamsburg, on the twenty-fifth day of April and twenty-
14 fifth day of October; for the county of New-Kent, on the tenth day
15 of May and tenth day of November; for the county of Charles
16 City, on the eighteenth day of May and eighteenth day of Novem-
17 ber; and for the county of Henrico, on the twenty-fifth day of May
18 and twenty-fifth day of November."

2. This act shall be in force from its passage.

SENATE BILL.

A BILL

To authorize the County Courts to arm the Militia of their respective Counties, and to provide means therefor.

1. Be it enacted by the General Assembly, That the county
2 courts of Charlotte county, and such other counties as may accept
3 the provisions of this act, as hereinafter provided; may arm such
4 portion of the militia of their respective counties as they may deem
5 expedient, and as may be without arms; provided, the authority
6 hereby given shall not be construed to impair any power over this
7 subject vested by law in the Governor.

2. For the purpose of paying the debt thus incurred, the court
2 shall have power to appoint an agent or agents to negotiate a loan or
3 loans for and in the name of such county, and at the term at which it
4 makes its county levy, shall levy on all the lands, and all other subjects
5 liable to that tax and county levy in such county, without the limits
6 of a town that provides for its poor and keeps its streets in order;
7 such tax to pay the said debt or part of such loan or loans as may be
8 authorized, and the interest thereon, as said court may deem neces-
9 sary and proper, and from year to year repeat such assessments,
10 until the amount authorized or loan made by such court, together

11 with all interest is fully paid. But such levy for a year shall not
12 exceed one-fifth of the whole amount of debt thus incurred at one
13 time.

3. The said courts shall not contract any debt or liability under
2 the provisions of this act, unless all the acting justices thereof shall
3 have been summoned to attend the court to consider the subject, and
4 a majority shall be present and consenting thereto.

4. This act shall apply to all counties wherein the county court,
2 the justices thereof having been summoned to consider the same,
3 and a majority being present, shall accept it.

5. This act shall be in force from its passage.

SENATE BILL.

A BILL

To protect the interest of the Commonwealth and other stockholders of Internal Improvement Companies in this State from injurious competition.

1. Be it enacted by the General Assembly, That it shall be law-
2 ful for any of the internal improvement companies in this State,
3 whose works constitute, together with the public works of another
4 State, the whole or a part of two competing lines of travel extend-
5 ing entirely through this State, in either of which lines this Com-
6 monwealth is interested as a stockholder, to purchase and hold, with
7 the consent of the Board of Public Works, the stock of any compa-
8 nies on such competing line to such extent as it may deem neces-
9 sary, to prevent injurious competition and a loss of remunerative
10 revenues to the Commonwealth, and the other stockholders of such
11 companies.

2. This act shall be in force from its passage.

BILL No. 22.

SENATE BILL.

A BILL

*To authorize the Norfolk and Petersburg railroad company to construct
a Branch and to increase its Capital Stock.*

1. Be it enacted by the General Assembly of Virginia, That it
2 shall be lawful for the Norfolk and Petersburg railroad company to
3 construct a branch of their road to some point on the North Caro-
4 lina line, with a view to connect with the proposed Edenton, or any
5 other railroad of North Carolina, whenever the stockholders of the
6 said company in general meeting shall authorize the same to be
7 done.

2. Be it further enacted, That it shall be lawful for the stock-
2 holders of the said company to increase the capital stock thereof,
3 by the sum of one hundred thousand dollars for and on account of
4 the construction of said branch road: provided however, that the
5 Board of Public Works shall subscribe for no part of such increased
6 capital stock.

3. This act shall be in force from its passage.

A BILL

*Allowing the Northwestern Bank of Virginia and any of its branches
to establish an agency in the city of Richmond for the redemption of
its circulating notes.*

1. Be it enacted by the General Assembly, That it shall be law-
2 ful for the parent bank or any branch of the Northwestern Bank of
3 Virginia to establish an agency in the city of Richmond for the
4 redemption of its circulating notes, at a rate of discount not exceed-
5 ing one-fourth of one per cent. If any such agency be established,
6 the president of the bank or branch shall certify the same to the
7 Governor of Virginia, with each quarterly report of the bank, and
8 such certificate shall be published with the report. For failure so
9 to certify such agency, the parent bank or branch establishing the
10 same, shall forfeit to the Commonwealth one hundred dollars for the
11 first offence, and five hundred dollars for each separate offence
12 thereafter.

2. It shall be the duty of the bank or branch establishing such
2 agency, to redeem on demand at such agency, at a rate of discount

3 not exceeding one-fourth of one per cent., all its circulating notes
4 which shall be presented at such agency for payment; and for a
5 failure so to redeem the same, the holder thereof may recover the
6 same damages, and in the same mode now provided for by law for
7 failure to pay in specie at the office or bank where payable.

    3. If the notes of the parent bank or branch which shall have
2 established such agency, be presented for redemption at the bank
3 or branch at which they are payable, such parent bank or branch
4 may redeem the same by a specie draft at par upon its agency at
5 Richmond, where it has made provision for the redemption of its
6 notes: provided, the aggregate amount of its notes presented and
7 held by the same persons shall exceed five hundred dollars. Any
8 person refusing to accept such draft in redemption of notes pre-
9 sented or held by him, shall not be entitled to proceed against such
10 bank or branch under the fifteenth section of the fifty-eighth chap-
11 ter of the Code.

    4. If the parent bank, or any branch of the Northwestern Bank
2 of Virginia, shall establish an agency in the city of Richmond, as
3 aforesaid, then so long as it shall continue to redeem its circulating
4 notes when presented for payment at such agency, at a rate of dis-
5 count not exceeding one-fourth of one per cent., it shall not be
6 subject to the act passed April 2, 1858, entitled "An act providing
7 for a more uniform currency of the banks of the State."

    5. The parent bank or branch establishing such agency, may

2 from time to time thereafter change the same, and appoint a new

3 agent for the purposes specified in this act; but every such appoint-

4 ment shall be forthwith certified as aforesaid to the Governor of

5 Virginia.

6. This act shall be in force from its passage.

BILL No. 32.

ↄ. 160
ₓ. 2287-8(?)

SENATE BILL.

A BILL

Authorizing the Superintendent of the Armory to provide quarters for a portion of the Public Guard.

1. Be it enacted by the General Assembly, That the Superin-
2 tendent of the Armory be authorized to rent temporarily, (subject
3 to the approval of the Governor,) quarters for such portion of the
4 Public Guard as it may be necessary to remove from the armory
5 buildings, in order to complete the repairs necessary for the manu-
6 facture of arms.

2. Be it further enacted, That a sum not exceeding

2 dollars be, and is hereby appropriated for the purpose of carrying
3 out the foregoing provision, to be paid, from time to time, upon the
4 order of the Governor, drawn upon the Auditor of Public Accounts.

3. This act shall be in force from its passage.

BILL No. 35.

SENATE BILL,

A BILL

To establish the Virginia Military Academy,

1. Be it enacted by the General Assembly, That there shall be
2 established, and maintained at some eligible point in the north-
3 western part of the State, a military school to be called the Vir-
4 ginia Military Academy.

  2. The sale of said academy shall be determined by three com-
2 missioners, or a majority of them, who shall be appointed by the
3 Governor of the Commonwealth. It shall be the duty of said com-
4 missioners, as soon as practicable after their appointment, to meet
5 on such day, and at such place in the said part of the State as the
6 Governor may specify ; and then and there, and at such other times
7 and places as they may deem proper, proceed as speedily as practi-
8 cable to select, and select the point most fit in all respects for the
9 site of the said academy, and shall report their proceedings and de-
10 termination to the Governor without delay. In case of the death,
11 refusal or inability to act, of any of said commissioners, the Gov-
12 ernor shall supply the vacancy thereby resulting, by appointment of
13 another or others as commissioners.

3. The said commissioners shall each receive four dollars per
2 day for every day they may be employed under this act.

4. When said commissioners shall have made the selection of the
2 site and report aforesaid, the Governor shall forthwith appoint a
3 board of visitors for said academy, consisting of nine persons, of
4 whom three shall be taken from the Trans-Alleghany, and two from
5 each of the other grand divisions of the State, to continue in office
6 one year; and annually thereafter, the Governor shall in like man-
7 ner appoint their successors for the same term.

5. The board of visitors aforesaid shall have authority to pur-
2 chase, hold, and use for said academy, not exceeding one hundred
3 acres of land, at a cost not exceeding $20,000, whereon to erect
4 said academy. It shall be the duty of said board to cause the
5 said academy to be built and completed for use as soon as practi-
6 cable.

6. The said board of visitors shall, as far as consistent with this
2 act, have all the power, and be subject to all the rules and restric-
3 tions of the board of visitors of the Virginia Military Institute,
4 under chapter thirty-four of the Code, and acts amendatory thereof,
5 as far as applicable.

7. For the purpose of carrying this act into execution, there is
2 hereby appropriated out of any money in the treasury not otherwise
3 appropriated, the sum of $100,000. The said visitors of the said
4 academy shall have power, from time to time, to order and direct
5 their treasurer to draw upon the treasurer of the Commonwealth,
6 which shall be audited by the Auditor of Public Accounts for such

7 part or parts of the said sum of $100,000 as may be necessary in
8 the execution of this act.

    8. When the said Virginia Military Academy shall be erected
2 and completed, it shall be paid the same annuity out of the Literary
3 fund as the Virginia Military Institute—to be paid in the same man-
4 ner, and on the same terms.

    9. This act shall be in force from its passage.

BILL No. 36.

SENATE BILL.

A BILL

To establish a State Board of Medical Examiners.

1. Be it enacted by the General Assembly of Virginia, That
2 from and after the   day of   , no person shall
3 be allowed to practice medicine or surgery, or any of the branches
4 thereof, or in any case prescribe for the cure of disease for fee or
5 reward, unless he or they shall have been first licensed to do so in
6 the manner hereinafter to be described.

2. If any such person shall, after this date, presume to practice
2 medicine or surgery, or any of the branches of either (dentistry
3 excepted), or in any manner to prescribe for the cure of disease for
4 fee or reward, he or they shall be liable to be indicted, and on con-
5 viction, fined the sum of five hundred dollars for every offense—one
6 half of the fine to enure to the informant, and the other to the treas-
7 ury of the Commonwealth.

3. On trial of all indictments for any of the offenses enume-
2 rated in this act, it shall be incumbent on the defendant to show that
3 he has been licensed to practice medicine or surgery, and to pre-
4 scribe for the cure of disease, in the manner hereinafter to be men-
5 tioned, to exempt himself from the penalties enumerated in this act.

4. All bonds, notes, promises and assumptions made to any
2 person or persons not licensed in the manner hereinafter mentioned,
3 the consideration of which shall be services rendered as a physician
4 or surgeon in prescribing for the cure of disease, shall and they are
5 hereby declared to be utterly void and of no effect.

5. In order to the proper regulation of the practice of medicine
2 and surgery, there shall be established a Board of Medical Exami-
3 ners, to consist of nine members, who shall hold their office for six
4 years, and shall be chosen in the following manner, to wit: one by
5 the medical department of the University of Virginia, one by the
6 Winchester medical school, and one by the Medical college of Vir-
7 ginia; of the remaining six, three shall be chosen by the Medical
8 society of Virginia, and three by the Governor of the Common-
9 wealth; said board to meet in the city of Richmond on the first
10 Monday in May, to conduct the examinations.

6. The said board of examiners shall examine, in all the branches
2 taught in the schools, all applicants for license to practice; and if,
3 on such examination, they be found competent, shall grant to such
4 applicants license to practice: provided, that seven members of the
5 board shall constitute a quorum: and provided, that five out of
6 seven be agreed on the qualification of such applicant: and pro-
7 vided, that such applicant shall have received a diploma from some
8 chartered or incorporated medical school or college, and shall be
9 twenty-one years of age, and can show evidence of a good moral
10 character; and the said board shall be entitled to demand and

11 receive of any applicant the sum of twenty dollars for such
12 examination.

7. The board of examiners be, and they are hereby authorized
2 and empowered to elect all such officers, and to frame all such by-
3 laws, as may be necessary to carry the law into effect, and in case
4 of death, removal, or refusal to act, of any member of said board,
5 the said board, or a quorum thereof, be, and they are hereby empow-
6 ered to fill such vacancies.

8. To prevent delay and inconvenience, two members of the
2 board may grant temporary license to applicants therefor, and make
3 report thereof to their next regular meeting for confirmation: pro-
4 vided, that such temporary license do not continue in force longer
5 than the next annual meeting of the board, and that a temporary
6 license shall in no case be granted by any two members of the board
7 after the applicant has been refused a license by the said examining
8 board.

9. No part or clause of this act shall have any operation or effect
2 upon any person who has been a *resident* practitioner of medicine or
3 surgery in this Commonwealth.

10. The board shall cause to be entered in a book, to be kept for
2 that purpose, the names of each and every person they shall license
3 to practice medicine and surgery, and the time of granting the same,
4 together with the names of the members of the board present, and
5 shall publish them in some newspaper in the city of Richmond
6 within thirty days after granting the same.

BILL No. 45.

SENATE BILL.

—

A BILL

To authorize Railroad Companies to appoint Police Agents.

1. Be it enacted by the General Assembly, That the president
2 of any railroad company incorporated by this State may, with the
3 approbation of the county court of any county through which the
4 road may pass, appoint a police agent or agents, who shall have
5 authority upon the road and other property within this State of
6 such company, to exercise all the powers which can lawfully be
7 exercised by any constable for the preservation of the peace, the
8 arrest of offenders and disorderly persons, and for the enforcement
9 of the laws against crimes; and such president may remove such
10 agents at his pleasure.

2. It shall be lawful for any such police agent, or for any per-
2 son in the employment of such company, to arrest any negro found
3 on such road, or any branch thereof, or any of the cars, works or
4 property of such company, without having proper written evidence
5 of the right of such negro to be there; and the person making such

6 arrest may deliver such negro to any jailor, or carry him or her

7 before any justice of the peace in this Commonwealth to be exam-

8 ined and committed to the proper custody, or otherwise dealt with

9 according to law.

     3. This act shall be in force from its passage.

BILL No. 47.

D. 10^d
Cy. 2287-12(D)

SENATE BILL.

———

A BILL

Increasing the number of permanent Clerks in the office of the Auditor of Public Accounts.

1. Be it enacted by the General Assembly, That the Auditor of
2 Public Accounts shall be authorized to appoint five additional clerks
3 in his office, to be numbered and known as the fifth, sixth, seventh,
4 eighth and ninth.

2. This act shall be in force from its passage.

—

A BILL

To provide more efficient Police regulations at the Poor-houses in this Commonwealth.

1. Be it enacted by the General Assembly, That the county
2 court or the judge of the circuit court of any county in which any
3 poor-house may be located, may upon the application of any super-
4 intendent of any such poor-house, or satisfactory evidence founded
5 on the information of others, that it is necessary, appoint some
6 citizen of the Commonwealth conservator of the peace, whose juris-
7 diction shall extend over the grounds attached to such poor-house,
8 and not exceeding one mile beyond the same, as shall be prescribed
9 by the order appointing said conservator.

2. This act shall be enforced from and after its passage.

A BILL

*To stay the proceedings on executions, trust deeds, and other demands,
in cases of refusal to receive bank notes.*

1. Be it enacted by the General Assembly, That no execution
2 or distress of any kind shall be levied, nor sale made under any
3 decree or order of any court, unless the party or parties, his, her or
4 their agent, attorney or representative, for whose benefit the money
5 is about to be made, shall authorize the officer or other person levy-
6 ing such execution or distress, or making such sale, to receive pay-
7 ment of the debt, interest and costs in the notes of the banks of
8 the Commonwealth, that may be at the time of such payment receiv-
9 able for taxes or other public dues.

2. And be it further enacted, That if any execution or distress
2 shall have been levied, but no sale made of the property taken,
3 before this act takes effect, the officer or person making such levy
4 shall not proceed to sell the property so taken unless he be author-
5 ized, as aforesaid, to receive in discharge of the debt, interest and
6 costs to be raised by such levy, the notes of the banks of this Com-
7 monwealth, that are or may be receivable for taxes and public dues:

8 and should such authority be not given after ten days' notice, to the

9 party or parties, his or her agent, attorney or representative, the

10 property so levied on shall be returned to the party from whose

11 possession it may have been taken : provided, however, that a new

12 execution or distress may thereafter be issued and levied in like

13 manner, as if no such levy had theretofore been made : provided, no

14 lien under existing laws shall be hereby affected.

3. And be it further enacted, That no sale shall be made under

2 any deed of trust unless the party or parties for whose benefit it is

3 about to be made, his, her or their agent, attorney or representative,

4 will agree upon such sale, to receive the notes of the banks afore-

5 said in discharge of the debt, interest and costs to be raised by such

6 sale; and if any such sale shall be made, the purchaser or purcha-

7 sers shall be entitled to discharge the purchase money by the pay-

8 ment of the notes of the banks aforesaid.

4. And be it further enacted, That all persons responsible for

2 any demands of the Commonwealth, and of the Board of Public

3 Works, and of the president and directors of the Literary fund, on

4 any judgment or decree, or for any fine, penalty or amercement,

5 or any recognizance, bond, contract or deed of trust, shall be, and

6 they are hereby authorized, during the continuance of this act, to

7 discharge any such demand, by the payment thereof in the notes of

8 the banks of this Commonwealth, that at the time of such payment

9 or tender of such payment, shall be receivable for taxes and other

10 public dues: provided, however, that all executions may be levied
11 and sales made as heretofore, if the security or securities for the
12 money due on said execution, desire the levy or sale, unless the
13 principal debtor shall enter into bond, with good security, payable to
14 the security or securities aforesaid, conditioned to indemnify him,
15 her or them against all loss that he, she or they may sustain, by
16 reason of his, her or their securityships for the money due on said
17 execution; and it shall be lawful for the sheriff or other officer to
18 take the bond aforesaid at any time before the sale under the execu-
19 tion; and upon the execution of said bond, he shall return the
20 property to the party, as is required in the second section of this
21 act, and return the bond to the officer from which the execution
22 issued, for the benefit of the said securities.

5. This act shall commence and be in force from the passing
2 thereof, and continue in force until   , in the
3 year 186   , and no longer.

SENATE BILL.

A BILL

Transferring the Huttonsville and Huntersville turnpike road to the counties through which the same passes.

1. Be it enacted by the General Assembly, That the Huttons-
2 ville and Huntersville turnpike road, from Huttonsville, in the
3 county of Randolph, to Marlam's Bottom, in the county of Poca-
4 hontas, be, and the same, together with the rights, franchises and
5 privileges, condemned, purchased and attaching thereto, are hereby
6 transferred to the counties through which the same passes—that is
7 to say, such part as may be in the county of Randolph, is surren-
8 dered and transferred to said county, and that part in the county of
9 Pocahontas, is surrendered and transferred to said county of Poca-
10 hontas.

2. Be it further enacted, That such parts of said road as may
2 be in either of said counties, shall be under the control of the county
3 courts of said counties; and the court of either of said counties
4 may cause the same to be kept in repair as other county roads are
5 kept in repair; or the said courts of either of said counties, may

6 continue and establish toll-gates for the collection of tolls, on such

7 parts of said road, not exceeding the rates now authorized by law,

8 to be collected, and to cause the same to be applied to repairs on

9 said road.

     3. This act shall be in force from its passage.

BILL No. 61.

P. 10¾ ½ ₂₅₇-16 [handwritten annotation]

SENATE BILL.

———

A BILL

To amend and re-enact the first and third sections of an act entitled, "An act to incorporate a company to construct, on the plan of James S. French, a railroad between Alexandria and Washington," passed February 27, 1854.

1. Be it enacted by the General Assembly, That it shall be
2. lawful to open books of subscription at the city of Alexandria,
3. under the direction of James S. French, John W. Maury, A. J.
4. Marshall, Cornelius Boyle, George French, Edgar Snowden and
5. R. W. Latham, or any two of them, and at such other places, under
6. the direction of such agents as a majority of the above named com-
7. missioners may appoint, for the purpose of receiving subscriptions
8. to an amount not exceeding three hundred thousand dollars, in
9. shares of one hundred dollars each, to constitute a joint capital
10. stock for constructing a railroad from the city of Alexandria, in
11. the State of Virginia, to the city of Washington, in the District
12. of Columbia, crossing the Potomac between, at some eligible point
13. between the two cities.

2. That all the proceedings of the Alexandria and Washington
2 railroad company, under the provisions of the said act, passed Feb-
3 ruary 27th, 1854, incorporating the said company, touching the
4 constructing and operating a railroad on the plan of James S.
5 French, are hereby declared legal and valid.

SENATE BILL.

A BILL

To incorporate the Parkersburg Bridge Company.

1. Be it enacted by the General Assembly, That it shall be law-
2 ful to open books to receive subscriptions to a capital stock not ex-
3 ceeding one million and a half of dollars, in shares of one hundred
4 dollars each, for the purpose of constructing a bridge over the Ohio
5 river at the town of Parkersburg, in the county of Wood. Said
6 books shall be opened at Parkersburg under the superintendence of
7 James Cook, John R. Murdoch, George Neal, jr., John A. Hutchin-
8 son and C. J. Neal, or any three of them; and at such other places,
9 and under the superintendence of such other agents, as the said com-
10 missioners may appoint.

2. Whenever fifty thousand dollars shall be subscribed, the sub-
2 scribers, their executors, administrators and assigns, shall be, and
3 they are hereby constituted a body politic and corporate, by the
4 name and style of the Parkersburg bridge company, subject to the
5 provisions of chapters fifty-six and fifty-seven of the Code of Vir-
6 ginia. The Northwestern Virginia railroad company, the Balti-

7 more and Ohio railroad company, and the Marietta and Cincinnati
8 railroad company, or either of them, may subscribe to the stock of
9 said company, and either of said companies may rent or lease said
10 bridge, after the same is constructed.

3. The company hereby incorporated may construct a bridge
2 across the Ohio river at the point above designated, for a railroad or
3 other purposes: provided, that the said bridge shall be so construct-
4 ed with a draw, or otherwise, that the same shall not in anywise
5 obstruct or impede the free navigation of said river for any kind of
6 boat or craft that usually navigates the same. It shall be lawful for
7 said company to establish rates of toll, which it may charge and
8 collect, on all locomotives, tenders, express, baggage, passenger and
9 burden cars, which may pass over said bridge, and for such freight,
10 passengers, persons, stock, or other thing, as may pass or be trans-
11 ported over said bridge: provided, that the rates of toll shall be
12 uniform and without discrimination as to all persons and things of
13 the same class, which may pass or be transported over the same.

4. This act shall be in force from its passage.

BILL No. 64.

———

A BILL

To protect the interests of this Commonwealth and others in railroad and steamboat companies in this State on the two lines between Baltimore and Weldon.

1. Be it enacted by the General Assembly, That it shall be law-
2 ful for any of the railroad and steamboat companies in this State,
3 constituting either of the two existing lines of through travel be-
4 tween Baltimore and Weldon, to purchase and hold with the assent
5 of the Board of Public Works the stock of any such company con-
6 stituting a part of the other of the said two competing lines to such
7 extent as it may deem expedient and necessary to prevent injurious
8 competition and a loss of remunerative revenues to the Common-
9 wealth and the other stockholders of such companies.

2. This act shall be in force from its passage.

BILL No. 65.

SENATE BILL.

A BILL

*To transfer a part of the Price's mountain and Cumberland Gap road
to the Mountain lake and Salt Sulphur springs turnpike company.*

1. Be it enacted by the General Assembly, That it shall be law-
2 ful for the Mountain lake and Salt Sulphur springs turnpike com-
3 pany, to adopt that portion of the Price's mountain and Cumberland
4 gap road lying between the residence of Enoch Atkins and the town
5 of Newport, as a part of their road, and to keep the same in proper
6 repair: provided, however, that before this act shall take effect, the
7 consent of the county court of Giles county shall be first obtained.

2. It shall not be lawful for the said Mountain lake and Salt
2 sulphur road to charge any toll between the present residence of
3 Enoch Atkins and the town of Newport, a distance of three miles,
4 and the consent hereby given may be withdrawn by the county court
5 of Giles, whenever the said company shall fail to keep said portion
6 of the road in repair, as required by the provisions of the Code of
7 Virginia in relation to county roads.

3. This act shall be in force from its passage.

BILL No. 70.

A BILL

Making railroad companies liable for damages in certain cases.

1. Be it enacted by the General Assembly, That the several
2 railroad companies of this State, and any other company whose road
3 or any part thereof may pass through any part of the territory of
4 this State, shall be liable to the owner of any live stock of any kind
5 that may be killed or injured on the said road, by the cars or engines
6 used or run thereon, for such damage as he may sustain by the
7 injury or destruction of such stock, to be recovered by action or
8 motion against such company, in the same manner as damages are
9 recovered in other cases: provided, that no company against which
10 damages have been assessed to fence in their road, shall be liable for
11 any stock killed belonging to the party in whose favor such damages
12 have been assessed, and upon such parcels of land as the said dam-
13 ages were meant to enclose, but which such party has failed to
14 enclose.

2. This act shall be in force from its passage.

BILL No. 72.

SENATE BILL.

A BILL

*To amend the sixth section of chapter 165 of the Code so as to allow
compensation to attorneys for the Commonwealth in the circuit courts
of towns and cities for services heretofore performed by them.*

1. Be it enacted by the General Assembly, That the sixth sec-
2 tion of chapter 165 of the Code of Virginia be amended and re-
3 enacted so as to read as follows:

4 "§ 6. There shall be elected by the voters in each county, an
5 attorney for the Commonwealth for each county court; and in each
6 county, city or town in which a circuit court is held, an attorney for
7 the Commonwealth in such court; and such election shall be held on
8 the same day in every fourth year, counting in each case from the
9 fourth Thursday in May 1852. The said elections shall be made
10 and vacancies in said offices shall be filled as prescribed in the
11 seventh chapter. The mode of ascertaining and certifying their elec-
12 tions, the commencement of their terms of office, their qualification
13 and the power to remove them, shall be according to the eighth chapter,
14 and the mode of contesting their elections shall be as provided in
15 the tenth chapter."

2. Be it further enacted, That the attorneys for the Common-
3 wealth in the circuit courts held for the cities and towns of this
4 Commonwealth for whom no compensation was provided by acts
5 heretofore passed, shall be entitled to receive the compensation al-
6 lowed by law to attorneys for the Commonwealth in other circuit
7 courts, for any services performed by them since the passage of the
8 act of 17th January 1860, to be ascertained by the certificates of
9 the said circuit courts.

3. This act shall be in force from its passage.

P. *Cr. 228.*

SENATE BILL.

———

A BILL

To increase the pay of certain Officers of the Public Guard.

1. Be it enacted by the General Assembly, That the third
2 section of chapter thirty-three of the Code be amended and re-
3 enacted so as to read as follows:

"§ 3. The pay per month of the said company shall be as
2 follows: Of the captain, sixty dollars; of the first lieutenant, fifty
3 dollars; of the second lieutenant, forty-five dollars; of the first
4 sergeant, twenty dollars; of each other sergeant, seventeen dollars;
5 of each corporal and musician, thirteen dollars; and of each private,
6 eleven dollars. Each noncommissioned officer, musician and private
7 shall receive one ration per day, in kind, and the same clothing and
8 quartermaster's stores as are allowed to infantry in the service of
9 the United States, under the laws and regulations thereof now in
10 force. Each of the commissioned officers shall be entitled to four
11 rations per day, to be commuted at thirty cents per ration, and
12 each shall be allowed, for one servant, the pay, rations and clothing
13 of a private, and such quartermaster's stores for himself and ser-
14 vant as are now allowed to the officers of the same grade in the
15 infantry of the United States."

2. This act shall be in force from its passage.

BILL No. 77.

—

A BILL

To increase the Capital Stock of the Richmond and York River Rail-

road Company.

1. Be it enacted by the General Assembly, That the capital

2 stock of the Richmond and York river railroad company be and is

3 hereby increased by the additional sum of one hundred thousand

4 dollars; and that the Board of Public Works be and is hereby

5 authorized to subscribe therefor and to borrow the necessary amount

6 in accordance with existing laws: provided, that no part of said

7 increased capital stock shall be paid by said Board, until the fact

8 has been duly certified to them that the stockholders in said com-

9 pany, in general meeting, have agreed to make and so ordered the

10 said increased capital hereby authorized, a preferred stock.

2. This act shall be in force from its passage.

BILL No. 77.

HOUSE BILL.

A BILL

Entitled "An act for the relief of the Banks of this Commonwealth."

With the amendments of the Senate, which are in *italics.*

---

1. Be it enacted by the General Assembly, That so much of all
2 or any acts as now may subject any bank or banking corporation
3 incorporated by the laws of this Commonwealth now in operation, or
4 which may be put in operation whilst this act is in force, to the for-
5 feiture of its charter or to any other penalty, for failing or refusing
6 to pay or redeem its notes or debts in specie, shall be and the same
7 are hereby suspended until the first day of March, eighteen hundred
8 and sixty-two; and if any such bank or banking corporation shall
9 have forfeited its charter by failing or refusing to pay in specie any
10 note or other debt due from such bank, the forfeiture thereby in-
11 curred shall be remitted; and the charter of such bank, with all the
12 rights and powers thereby conferred, except such portions thereof
13 as are hereinbefore suspended, shall be and the same is hereby
14 declared to be in full force and effect, to all intents and purposes,
15 until the date before mentioned: provided, that nothing herein con-
16 tained shall be so construed as to prevent the recovery of the amount

17 of any note or debt due from any such bank, with legal interest
18 thereon, in the mode prescribed by law.

2. The notes of the several banks which have been heretofore
2 required to be received in payment of taxes and debts due to the
3 Commonwealth, shall continue to be so received, and the deposits of
4 the public revenue shall continue to be made in the banks now
5 authorized by law to receive the same, until the period hereinbefore
6 mentioned, unless the Treasurer, with the advice of the Executive,
7 shall direct otherwise in respect to such receipts or deposits, or both,
8 in the mode prescribed by law.

3. Nothing in this act shall be so construed as to prevent any
2 of the banks of this Commonwealth from resuming specie payment
3 at any time prior to the date hereinbefore mentioned, at the discre-
4 tion of the president and directors thereof.

4. Be it further enacted, That sections one, two, three and four
2 of the act passed April second, eighteen hundred and fifty-eight,
3 providing for a more uniform currency of the banks of the State, be
4 and the same are hereby repealed.

5. *It shall be the duty of the several banks and branch banks of*
2 *the State whenever required by the Governor, to redeem in specie or*
3 *specie funds, such an amount of their notes as may be necessary to*
4 *meet the specie demands upon the treasury of the Commonwealth and*
5 *to this end the contribution shall be rateable and in proportion to the*
6 *amount of the notes on each bank or branch bank, which may be re-*
7 *ceived by the Treasurer in payment of public revenue.*

6. *On the payment of every note, bill or draft payable at the cities*
2 *of Baltimore, Philadelphia, New York or Boston, heretofore dis-*
3 *counted by and which is now unpaid and the property of any bank*
4 *or branch, or which may be hereafter discounted by any bank or*
5 *branch during the suspension of specie payment by it, such bank or*
6 *branch shall pay to the party for whom such paper was discounted,*
7 *the excess of exchange at the time of such payment over and above*
8 *the rate between the point where such bank or branch is located and*
9 *the point where such paper is payable, at the time such bank or*
10 *branch suspended specie payment; and on failure of such bank or*
11 *branch to pay such excess on paper hereafter discounted, the party*
12 *entitled thereto may recover the same by warrant before any justice*
13 *of the peace, or when the amount is over fifty dollars, by motion*
14 *on ten days' notice before any court of the county or corporation*
15 *where such bank or branch is located; and on the failure of any*
16 *bank or branch to pay such excess on paper heretofore discounted*
17 *and unpaid as aforesaid, such bank or branch shall not have the*
18 *benefit of the provisions of this act releasing any penalty or forfeit-*
19 *ure incurred by it by the nonpayment of specie.*

7. *The thirty-third section of chapter fifty-eighth of the Code of*
2 *Virginia, shall be amended and re-enacted so as to read as follows:*
3 *"§16. Any bank authorized to carry on business as a bank of cir-*
4 *culation, deposit and discount, may loan money for a period not ex-*
5 *ceeding six months, and discount any bill of exchange, promissory*
6 *note or other negotiable paper for the payment of money which will*

7   *be payable within six months from the time of discounting the same.*

8   *A bank may take interest on its loans and discounts at the rate of one*

9   *half of one per centum for thirty days, and the interest may be re-*

10 *ceived in advance. Each bank or branch shall so regulate its loans*

11 *and discounts that the same shall not, together with what it may have*

12 *paid for stock of this State and bonds guaranteed by this State, ex-*

13 *ceed twice the amount of capital actually paid into such bank or*

14 *allotted to such branch.*

15 *Any President, Director or Cashier who may be instrumental in*

16 *violating this section shall be fined   dollars.*

       8. *No bank or branch of a bank which may have been heretofore*

2   *incorporated or authorized to be established by the General Assem-*

3   *bly, and which shall not at the time that this act takes effect, have*

4   *actually gone into legal operation, according to the terms of its*

5   *charter, shall be permitted to do so during the suspension of specie*

6   *payments by the banks of this Commonwealth. But this section*

7   *shall not be construed to apply to amended charters of Banks now*

8   *in operation: provided that this section shall not apply to the Bank*

9   *of the city of Petersburg.*

       9. This act shall be in force from its passage.

A BILL

To amend an act entitled, "An act to incorporate the Richmond and York river railroad company," passed January 31, 1853.

1. Be it enacted by the General Assembly, That the first section
2 of the act, entitled, "An act to incorporate the Richmond and York
3 river railroad company," passed the 31st of January, 1853, be
4 re-enacted and amended so as to read as follows:

5   "§1. Be it enacted by the General Assembly of Virginia, That
6 it shall be lawful to open books in the city of Richmond, and in such
7 other place or places as the commissioners hereinafter named shall
8 think fit, under the direction of Edward J. Wilson, Bernard Peyton,
9 R. B. Haxall, Robert S. Apperson, James Lyons, R. H. Maury, C.
10 Dimmock, Abraham Warwick, James Stamper and John D. Chris-
11 tian, or any three of the same, or any deputies or agents of the said
12 commissioners, for the purpose of receiving subscriptions to an
13 amount not less than two hundred and fifty thousand dollars nor
14 more than five hundred thousand dollars, in shares of one hun-
15 dred dollars each, for the purpose of constructing a railroad from
16 the city of Richmond to some point on York river, or near the

17 mouth of Pamunkey river, and providing everything necessary and

18 convenient for the transportation on the said road; and that the

19 said railroad company be, and is hereby authorized to make such

20 connections with steamboat lines, and other lines of navigation or

21 transportation, as may, in the opinion of the directory of the said

22 company, be conducive to its success and prosperity.

SENATE BILL.

A BILL

To incorporate the American Agency.

1. Be it enacted by the General Assembly, That Duff Green,
2 James Lyons, John S. Barbour, Jeptha Fowlkes and J. Robin
3 McDaniel, and the owners of the shares herein authorized to be
4 issued, be and they are hereby made a body politic and corporate,
5 under the name and style of the "American Agency," with power and
6 authority in that name and style to contract and be contracted with,
7 to sue and be sued, to plead and be impleaded, with all the rights,
8 powers and privileges which may be necessary or proper for them
9 to have, possess and exercise as an incorporated company, and
10 especially to take, have, possess and acquire by gift, grant or pur-
11 chase, any property and estate, real or personal, and the same to
12 use, lease, let, mortgage, sell, transfer and convey in as full and
13 ample manner as any individual may or might do.

2. Whereas one purpose of this act is to organize an incorpo-
2 rated company, with the intent and purpose of aiding in the purchase
3 and sale of railroad bonds and shares, and other public and private
4 securities, therefore the said company may and they are hereby

2   Bill No. 84.

5 authorized and empowered to receive and hold on deposit and in
6 trust, any property and estate, real and personal, including the
7 shares of railroad and other improvement companies, and the notes,
8 bonds, accounts and obligations of governments, states, cities, towns,
9 counties, corporations, companies and individuals, and the same may
10 purchase, collect, adjust and settle, and they may sell and dispose
11 thereof in any market in the United States or elsewhere, without
12 proceeding in law or in equity, and upon such terms and for such
13 price as may be agreed upon between them and the parties contract-
14 ing with them; and may deal in exchange, foreign and domestic;
15 and may make advances of money and of credit, and may endorse
16 and guarantee the payment of the notes and bonds and the perform-
17 ance of the obligations of governments, and of states, cities, towns,
18 counties, corporations, companies and individuals, and may charge
19 and receive such commissions and premiums as may be agreed upon
20 between them and the parties contracting with them.

    3. The persons named in section one, or a majority of them,
2 may, in person or by proxy, open books of subscription at such
3 times and places as they may deem expedient, and when three hun-
4 dred thousand dollars shall be subscribed, the shareholders may
5 organize the company by the election of five or more directors; and
6 the directors for the time being, shall have power, in the name and
7 behalf of the company, to enact by-laws and regulations for the
8 management of their affairs, and to exercise and enjoy all the rights,
9 powers and privileges herein granted, and which it may be necessary

10 or proper for them as such to have, exercise and enjoy; and they
11 may from time to time enlarge the resources of the company by
12 borrowing money on a pledge of their property and estate, or with-
13 out such pledge, or by new subscriptions; and any citizen or subject
14 corporation or company, of any government, state or country may
15 subscribe for, purchase and hold shares of the said company, subject
16 to no other liability on account thereof than for the payment to the
17 said company of the sums due or to become due on the shares sub-
18 scribed for or held by them.

4. The by-laws may prescribe the manner in which the directors,
2 officers and agents of the company shall be selected, and may also
3 define their powers and duties, and fix their term of service and
4 compensation. The company shall have an office in the city of
5 Richmond, and the directors for the time being may from time to
6 time establish such branches and agencies in Europe and elsewhere
7 as they may deem expedient, under such rules and regulations as
8 they may prescribe; and divide the capital of the company into
9 shares, and prescribe the manner in which they shall be transferred
10 on the books of the company. And the said company shall not
11 issue their own notes or bills to be used as bank notes or as cur-
12 rency, nor shall their by-laws or regulations be inconsistent with the
13 laws or constitution of this State.

5. This act shall be in force from its passage, and shall be sub-
2 ject to amendment, modification or repeal at the pleasure of the
3 General Assembly.

BILL No. 89.

SENATE BILL.

———

A BILL

Concerning the Court of Appeals and the Special Court of Appeals.

Whereas, in consequence of the great accumulation of civil

2 causes upon the docket of the court of appeals, occasioned in part

3 by the exercise of the appellate jurisdiction in criminal causes, con-

4 ferred upon it by the first section of the act regulating the jurisdic-

5 tion of the district courts and court of appeals, passed 5th June,

6 1852, it is manifestly impracticable for that court, by its own

7 unaided efforts, however strenuous and unremitting, and without

8 some legislative interposition and relief, ever to bring up the arrear-

9 age, and at the same time dispose of their annually accruing current

10 business, with that expedition and despatch so vitally important in

11 the administration of justice: and whereas, the most expedient and

12 practicable remedy for the evil of delay, which is recommended to

13 the adoption of the General Assembly, is a scheme of relief similar

14 to that adopted by the act of the 10th March, 1848, establishing

15 and conferring upon a special court of appeals both civil and crimi-

16 nal appellate jurisdiction, which shall consist in continuing the exis-

17 tence of the present special court of appeals, holden in the city of
18 Richmond, and transferring to it the appellate criminal jurisdiction
19 now exercised by the court of appeals, together with an annual
20 docket of civil causes, as was done by the last mentioned act of the
21 10th March, 1848:

1. Be it therefore enacted by the General Assembly, That there
2 shall be a special court of appeals, and the said court shall be com-
3 posed of one judge from each judicial section of the State, and the
4 judge from such section shall be selected by the district courts first
5 held after the passage of this act, for the purpose of receiving and
6 exercising the appellate jurisdiction, civil and criminal, conferred
7 by the subsequent sections and clauses of this act, as well as for
8 performing the functions required by the act passed February 25,
9 1854, entitled, "An act for forming a special court of appeals," &c.

2. That all the appellate jurisdiction in criminal cases conferred
2 on the court of appeals, by the first section of the act mentioned in
3 the preamble, passed June 5, 1852, being all the appellate jurisdic-
4 tion in criminal cases theretofore exercised by the general court,
5 and by any subsequent enactment, be, and the same is hereby taken
6 away from the court of appeals, and transferred to the special court
7 of appeals, so that the said special court of appeals and the judges
8 thereof, shall respectively succeed to and have and exercise all the
9 appellate jurisdiction in criminal causes now in virtue of existing
10 laws, vested in, exercised or exercisable by the court of appeals or
11 the judges thereof.

3. That the special court of appeals shall hereafter hold two
2 terms in every year, at the State courthouse, in the city of Rich-
3 mond, instead of one as now required by law, commencing on the
4 first Monday in July and first Monday in January, and that the
5 next of said terms shall commence on the first Monday of July
6 next. The court shall be attended by the same officers, who shall
7 perform the same duties and receive the same compensation as those
8 now attending the court, save and except that the court shall make
9 to the clerk of the court of appeals, for his ex officio services here-
10 after performed in said court, and for which heretofore no compen-
11 sation was authorized by law, a reasonable per diem allowance. The
12 July term shall be devoted to the exercise of its appellate criminal
13 jurisdiction. The January term to both the criminal and the civil—
14 first the criminal and then the civil: but nothing herein contained
15 shall preclude the court from deciding civil causes at the July terms
16 if found practicable and desired by the parties litigant.

4. Hereafter, writs of error from the special court of appeals to
2 a circuit court in any criminal case, may be awarded in term time,
3 or by any judge thereof in vacation, who did not preside at the trial
4 of the case, as by the existing law may now be done by a judge of
5 the court of appeals; and no writ of error or supersedeas to or
6 appeal from any judgment, order or decree of a circuit court in a
7 civil case, cognizable in the court of appeals, shall be awarded by a
8 judge of the circuit courts or such judge, or judge of the district
9 courts or special court of appeals: but the same shall be granted or

10 allowed only by the court of appeals in term time, or a judge thereof
11 in vacation.

    5. The court of appeals shall hereafter annually, at or near the
2 close of their last term next preceding the first Monday in January,
3 cause a docket to be made out by their clerk, of the causes depend-
4 ing on their docket, to be assigned and transmitted to the special
5 court of appeals for decision at the January term succeeding of said
6 special court. Such of these causes as shall be undecided at the
7 close of such term, shall, after the adjournment of said court, be
8 replaced on the docket of the court of appeals, and thereafter called,
9 heard and disposed of, so far as practicable, in the order of pri-
10 ority of call and hearing to which they were entitled before their
11 transfer, unless by consent of parties they shall be permitted to
12 remain and retain their places upon the docket of the special court.

    6. In order to determine and designate the causes which shall
2 be placed on the docket mentioned in the preceding section for hear-
3 ing and decision by the special court, the court of appeals shall
4 cause its docket to be called on a day assigned for the purpose, after
5 notice thereof given to the counsel practising in the court, begin-
6 ning the call with the causes of longest standing on the docket, and
7 coming down until a docket of causes is obtained wherein the parties
8 or their counsel, either expressly consent to or make no objection to
9 the transfer; and if a docket cannot be so obtained, in whole or in
10 part, it shall be the duty of the court to form the entire docket, or
11 supply the deficiency, as the case may be, from the causes on their

12 docket of longest standing, without consent, either expressed or
13 implied, from a failure to object, and if necessary, against the con-
14 sent of the parties litigant.

7. All causes involving the exercise of its appellate criminal
2 jurisdiction, remaining on the docket of the court of appeals on the
3 first day of July next, shall be transferred to the docket of the
4 special court of appeals for decision.

8. It shall be the duty of the reporter to the court of appeals
2 to report, in his annual volume of reports, all the decisions of the
3 special court in criminal cases, and such of their decisions in civil
4 cases as the court shall order and direct.

9. All acts and parts of acts coming within the purview of this
2 act, are hereby repealed.

10. This act shall be in force from and after the first day of July
2 next.

A BILL

To authorize an issue of preferred stock by the Alexandria, Mount
Vernon and Accotink turnpike company.

1. Be it enacted by the General Assembly of Virginia, That it
2 shall be lawful for the stockholders of the Alexandria, Mount Ver-
3 non and Accotink turnpike company, in general meeting assembled,
4 to make the stock of said company to the extent of twelve thousand
5 dollars, a preferred stock, by guaranteeing a dividend of six per
6 centum per annum for a fixed or indefinite period on each share of
7 stock so preferred, payable out of the net proceeds of said road.
8 And, whereas, it is represented to the General Assembly that the
9 said turnpike company, under a mistaken apprehension of their
10 powers under their charter, have already issued certificates of stock
11 preferred as aforesaid, amounting to the sum of five thousand dol-
12 lars, which said certificates are now in the hands of bona fide holders
13 for value.

2. Be it further enacted, That it shall be lawful to make up the
2 amount of preferred stock hereinbefore authorized, as well by con-
3 firming and ratifying the preferred issue already made, as by the
4 issue of new certificates, and in the event of such confirmation and

5 ratification, the said certificates so confirmed and ra ied shall there-
6 upon become legalized as fully and to all interests nd purposes as
7 if authorized by law at the date of their issue.

3. Be it further enacted, That if the said pref red stock shall
2 be made up by the issue of new certificates before suing the same
3 or any portion thereof to any other person, it sha be the duty of
4 said company to redeem and replace the preferred ce ificates already
5 issued by the new certificates to be issued under thority of this
6 act, or to reserve and retain a sufficiency thereof fo hat purpose.

4. This act shall be in force from the date of it passage.

SENATE BILL.

A BILL

To amend an a. entitled, "An act to incorporate the Farmville and Buckingh i plank road company," passed May 22, 1852.

1. Be ii iacted by the General Assembly, That the second sec-
2 tion of an a passed May 22, 1852, entitled, "An act to incorporate
3 the Farmvill and Buckingham plank road company," be amended
4 and re-enae: l so as to read as follows:

2. Wl.e ive thousand shares of the stock shall have been sub-
2 scribed, th subscribers, their executors, administrators or assigns,
3 shall be inc porated into a company by the name and style of "the
4 Farmville ani Buckingham plank road company," agreeably to the
5 provision o the fifty-seventh and sixty-first chapters of the Code
6 of Virginia provided, that the said road shall be graded at least
7 twenty feet ide and constructed with plank at least eight feet wide,
8 and that its rade shall nowhere exceed four degrees, and that the
9 same may l repaired when necessary with stone, dirt, gravel or
10 other matei l at the discretion of the board of directors.

3. This ct shall be in force from its passage.

BILL No. 93.

SENATE BILL.

———

A BILL

Providing that railroad companies in which the Commonwealth is a stockholder, shall use in the construction, equipment, repair and operation of their roads, materials, supplies, machinery and other fabrics produced and manufactured in this State.

1. Be it enacted by the General Assembly, That it shall be the
2 duty of every railroad company in which the Commonwealth is a
3 stockholder, and of the Board of Public Works, representing the
4 interest of the Commonwealth in railroads owned entirely by the
5 Commonwealth, to use in the construction, equipment, repair and
6 operations of their roads, materials, supplies, machinery and other
7 fabrics which have been produced and manufactured in this Com-
8 monwealth, in every instance, when such material, supplies, machine-
9 ry and other fabrics, produced and manufactured in this Common-
10 wealth, can be obtained at a reasonable cost; and when it shall be
11 necessary to use articles produced and manufactured in foreign
12 countries, it shall be the duty of said railroad companies in which
13 the Commonwealth is a stockholder, and of the Board of Public
14 Works, to use only, if practicable, articles which may have been
15 imported directly into this Commonwealth.

2. For the purpose of securing the production and manufacture
2. in this Commonwealth, of materials, supplies, machinery and other
3 fabrics, needed in the construction, equipment, repair and operation
4 of railroads, the railroad companies of this State are authorized to
5 aid, with their corporate funds, in the erection and establishment of
6 factories in this State for the production and manufacture of such
7 materials, supplies and other fabrics.

3. It shall be the duty of the Board of Public Works to instruct
2 the president and directors representing the interest of the Com-
3 monwealth in railroad companies, to carry into effect this act; and
4 it shall also be the duty of the Board of Public Works, to remove
5 from office any State director or proxy who shall fail or refuse to
6 aid by all proper means in the execution of this act.

4. This act shall be in force from its passage.

D.
123
Ca. 2287-31

SENATE BILL.

A BILL

To organize a volunteer force to be called the Virginia Volunteer Legion.

1. Be it enacted by the General Assembly, That the Governor
2 of the Commonwealth be and he is hereby authorized to organize a
3 volunteer division, the same to be constituted as hereinafter pro-
4 vided, to be composed of such companies of the volunteer force of
5 the State as are now in existence, or shall hereafter be organized,
6 which may offer their services to the Governor for this object, and
7 if necessary, of such additional companies as he may designate;
8 this force to be known as the Virginia Volunteer Legion.

2. The legion shall consist of one major general, two brigadier
2 generals, twelve regiments of infantry and riflemen, two regiments
3 of cavalry, one corps of artillery sufficient to man ten batteries of
4 four pieces each, and one company of engineer troops, together with
5 such general and regimental staff officers as may be necessary to
6 complete the organization.

3. Each regiment of infantry and riflemen shall be composed of
2 one colonel, one lieutenant colonel, one major, ten companies aver-
3 aging 65 men, including officers, one adjutant with the rank of first
4 lieutenant, one surgeon with the assimilated rank of major, one

5 assistant surgeon with the assimilated rank of captain, one regi-
6 mental quartermaster and commissary with the rank of first lieuten-
7 ant, one sergeant major, and one quartermaster's and commissary's
8 sergeant.

4. Each regiment of cavalry shall consist of one colonel, one
2 lieutenant colonel, one major, five squadrons of 120 men each, in-
3 cluding officers, each squadron to be composed of two companies,
4 one adjutant with the rank of first lieutenant, one surgeon with the
5 assimilated rank of major, one assistant surgeon with the assimi-
6 lated rank of captain, one regimental quartermaster and commissary,
7 one sergeant major, and one quartermaster's and commissary's ser-
8 geant.

5. The corps of artillery shall consist of one colonel, one lieu-
2 tenant colonel, one major, and ten companies of not less than 85
3 men each, including officers.

6. The company of engineer troops shall consist of 85 men,
2 including officers.

7. The general and field officers shall be appointed by the Gov-
2 ernor, with the advice and consent of the Senate, to hold office
3 during good behavior, or until such time as in the opinion of the
4 Governor it is no longer necessary to keep up the legion as a sepa-
5 rate organization.

8. The major general shall be entitled to the services of one
2 assistant adjutant general with the rank of major, and two aids-de-
3 camp with the rank of captain; three staff officers to be appointed

4 by the Governor, on the recommendation of the major general.

5 Each Brigadier general shall be entitled to the services of one

6 assistant adjutant general with the rank of captain, and one aid-de-

7 camp with the rank of first lieutenant; three staff officers to be

8 appointed by the Governor, on the recommendation of the brigadier

9 generals.

9. It shall be the duty of the adjutant general to assign the

2 companies to regiments as their services are tendered, and as the

3 latter are filled up, to notify the colonels of the same, and inform

4 them of the places of rendezvous of the companies.

10. It shall be the duty of the colonel of each regiment, so

2 soon as he is furnished with a list of the companies of his regiment

3 and their places of rendezvous, to make a tour of inspection, for

4 the purpose of seeing that his companies are all properly uniformed,

5 armed and equipped, and that they are in all respects ready for

6 immediate active service; and for the purpose of defraying his ex-

7 penses while on such tour, he shall be entitled to transportation at

8 the rate of ten cents per mile, estimated by the shortest mail route

9 between the places visited.

11. It shall be the duty of the major general to require the

2 companies which compose the legion to assemble at stated times for

3 the purposes of drill and instruction in the field. First, they shall

4 assemble in separate battalions or regiments at convenient points;

5 each regiment or battalion in command of its colonel or other field

6 officer, whose duty it shall be to exercise it as frequently as possible

7 in the evolutions of the battalion. Second, two or more regiments
8 or battalions shall be concentrated at the point most convenient for
9 assembling the whole, in command of the brigadier general of the
10 brigade to which the regiments are attached, for instruction in the
11 evolutions of the line, and such other instruction as the command-
12 ing officer may deem necessary.

12. It shall be the duty of the railroad companies in which the
2 State is a stockholder, to transport free of charge the companies
3 and officers constituting the legion, with their baggage and equip-
4 ments, when ordered into service for drill or otherwise, and the
5 Board of Public Works shall instruct the proxies and directors rep-
6 resenting the State in the railroad companies, to carry into effect
7 this section.

BILL No. 102.

A BILL

To amend the act to amend the pilot laws in regard to the Potomac river, passed March 20, 1860.

1. Be it enacted by the General Assembly, That the first sec-
2 tion of the above mentioned act be repealed and re-enacted so as to
3 read as follows:

4   "§1. That the county court of Alexandria county shall appoint
5 five suitable persons to constitute a board of commissioners to ex-
6 amine persons applying for branches as pilots for the river Potomac.
7 The said board, when appointed, shall meet at Alexandria, and shall
8 continue in office for three years from the dates of their appoint-
9 ment, respectively. Every person applying to said board to be
10 licensed as a branch pilot shall satisfy them of his citizenship and
11 of his good character, and the said board shall not appoint or license
12 any person unless they are fully satisfied that he is qualified by ser-
13 vice and experience to act as a pilot for the Potomac river. Said
14 board shall take bond with good and sufficient surety from every
15 person they may license as such pilot, in the penalty of five hundred
16 dollars for the faithful discharge of his duty, which they shall re-

17 turn to the clerk of the county court of Alexandria county, to be
18 by him filed. They shall be allowed a fee of five dollars for each
19 person they shall so license. The said bonds shall be renewed every
20 year, and the bond shall from time to time decide how many pilots
21 are necessary.

2. Be it further enacted, That the third section of said act be
2 repealed and re-enacted so as to read as follows:

3　§3. "The said pilots are authorized to receive and collect from ves-
4 sels bound to or from sea, pilotage at the following rates, viz: on
5 licensed coasting vessels of less than four hundred tons measurement,
6 seven cents per ton, and not more than one dollar and seventy-five cents
7 per foot up, and one dollar and fifty cents per foot down the river
8 on all other vessels for the entire distance between a point bearing
9 southwest from Point Lookout and Alexandria, and every vessel
10 spoken by such a pilot between said point and Ragged Point, or at
11 Alexandria, and refusing him, shall pay one dollar and twenty-five
12 cents: provided, that British American vessels owned in the British
13 provinces or in the United States bound to the port of Alexandria
14 from any of said provinces, or from Alexandria to the same, shall
15 be subject only to the same charges for pilotage and shall be on the
16 same footing in regard to pilotage as vessels belonging to citizens of
17 the United States sailing under coasting license, and provided also,
18 that it shall be lawful for all vessels engaged in the coal trade to
19 proceed from or to any place in this State without any charge for
20 pilotage, and should satisfactory evidence be afforded that any ves-

21 sel is bound to such place in ballast for the purpose of carrying coal,

22 such vessel shall be free from pilotage, both inward and outward

23 bound: and provided further, that all claims accruing under this

24 act shall be recoverable with costs before any justice of the peace

25 of Alexandria county, or court of said county having jurisdiction

26 and not otherwise.

BILL No. 105.

SENATE BILL.

A BILL

To authorize the sale of a portion of the armory grounds, and out of the proceeds thereof to purchase a site for an arsenal and quarters for the public guard, and to erect buildings for that purpose.

1. Be it enacted by the General Assembly, That the Governor
2 be, and is hereby required to sell so much of the armory grounds,
3 as in the opinion of the superintendent of the armory and the mas-
4 ter armorer, can be dispensed with without interfering with the
5 efficient operations of the armory as a manufactory of arms.

2. Be it further enacted, That the Governor be, and he is hereby
2 required to purchase suitable grounds in or near the city of Rich-
3 mond, and to erect thereupon suitable buildings for the public guard
4 and for storing arms and munitions of war belonging to the State:
5 provided, the whole cost for grounds and buildings shall not exceed
6 the sum obtained for the sale of said armory grounds.

3. Be it further enacted, That the Governor be, and he is hereby
2 authorized to exercise his discretion as to the time and manner of
3 sale of the said armory grounds, and to anticipate the said sale by
4 proceeding at once in erecting said buildings.

4. This act shall be in force from its passage.

SENATE BILL.

A BILL

For the protection of the fisheries on the waters of the Potomac river and Chesapeake bay.

1. Be it enacted by the General Assembly, That from and after
2 the passage of this act, it shall be unlawful for any person, not a
3 resident of this State, to fish with trot lines in any of the waters of
4 the Potomac river or Chesapeake bay, within this State.

    2. That upon complaint being made on oath by any competent
2 person, before any justice of the peace of any county in this State,
3 that any person or persons who do not reside in Virginia, have set
4 trot lines for fishing in any water lying wholly or partly in such
5 county, contrary to the provisions of this act, it shall be the duty of
6 such justice to issue his warrant, directed to the sheriff or any con-
7 stable of such county, commanding him to forthwith take possession
8 of such fishing lines, and to summon the owner or owners thereof to
9 appear before him, at some time and place to be designated in such
10 warrant, to answer the charge of such unlawful fishing. The said
11 justice shall examine such witnesses as may be produced, either by
12 the party complaining or the party complained of, and if it shall

13 satisfactorily appear to such justice, that the complaint is true, he
14 shall cause the said trot lines to be destroyed, and adjudge the
15 offending party to pay the cost of such proceeding. If it shall
16 appear that such complaint was improperly made, the party com-
17 plaining shall be adjudged to pay all costs occasioned thereby, and
18 shall be further liable for damages to any party injured by any such
19 seizure.

    3. Any party offending against the provisions of this act, by
2 such unlawful fishing, shall, in addition to the penalties and forfeit-
3 ures prescribed by the preceding section, be fined not less than fifty
4 nor more than five hundred dollars.

    4. This act shall be in force from its passage.

BILL No. 111.

SENATE BILL.

A BILL

Appropriating a sum of money to purchase certain ordnance and material of J. L. Archer of Bellona foundry, in this State.

1. Be it enacted by the General Assembly, That the Governor
2 of Virginia be, and he is hereby authorized and directed to contract
3 immediately with J. L. Archer of the Bellona foundry, in this State,
4 for all the guns, shot, shell and material of war made by him, and
5 now in his possession, to be used for the defenses of this State.

2. That the sum of thirty thousand three hundred and twenty-
2 two dollars and eighty cents, be, and the same are hereby appro-
3 priated for the purchase of the said guns, shot, shell and material of
4 war, as follows: thirteen thousand twenty-four dollars to be paid
5 out of any money now in the treasury not otherwise appropriated,
6 and the balance out of the fund heretofore appropriated for the pur-
7 chase of arms.

3. This act shall be in force from its passage.

SENATE BILL.

A BILL

Authorizing the Governor to Commission and Arm "Home Guards" as independent military organizations.

Whereas, it is represented that there are large numbers of
2 our citizens, in different sections of the State, over the age of forty-
3 five years, and not subject to militia duty, who are desirous of form-
4 ing themselves into military companies, for the purpose of protecting
5 the property, homes and lives of the people, and acting in the
6 capacity of "Home Guards" in the present crisis:

1. Be it enacted by the General Assembly, That the Governor
2 be and is hereby authorized, as soon as he shall receive the certifi-
3 cate of the commandant of any regiment, that such a company is
4 duly organized within the bounds of such regiment, with not less
5 than forty-five members, rank and file, and setting forth the names
6 of the officers elected, to issue commissions accordingly, and to
7 furnish such company with necsssary arms and equipments upon
8 their complying with the requirements of the law in relation thereto.

2. The said companies shall constitute independent military
2 organizations, and shall be subject to duty under their own officers,

3 and only within the limits of their respective counties or corpora-
4 tions. A majority of the members of any such companies may
5 adopt such by-laws as may be necessary for its government, not in
6 conflict with the constitution and laws of the United States or of
7 this Commonwealth.

   3. The right is hereby reserved to the Governor, for good cause
2 in his opinion, to withdraw the commissions issued under this act,
3 and to disband such companies.

   4. This act shall be in force from its passage.

SENATE BILL.

A BILL

Incorporating the Southern institution for the amelioration of the condition of the deaf, dumb and blind negroes of the Commonwealth.

1. Be it enacted, That William M. Langhorne and such other per-
2 sons as may or shall be hereafter associated with him, be constituted
3 a body politic and corporate under the name and style of "the
4 Southern institution for the amelioration of the condition of the
5 deaf, dumb and blind negroes," and by that name shall have perpet-
6 ual succession, may sue, and be sued, plead and be impleaded, have
7 and use a common seal, and be subject to all the provisions of chap-
8 ter   of the Code of Virginia, so far as they may be applicable
9 to this act.

2. The said company shall have power to purchase lands for the
2 purpose of said institution not exceeding in quantity fifty acres, and
3 other property not exceeding in value fifty thousand dollars.

3. The said institution shall be managed by such officers and
2 directors as a majority of those interested may appoint, and shall be
3 governed by such by-laws as may be adopted by them not inconsist-
4 ent with the constitution or laws of this State.

4. This act shall be in force from its passage.

BILL No. 118.

HOUSE BILL.

A BILL

Imposing taxes for the support of government.

With amendments proposed by Senate Committee on Finance and Claims.

1. Be it enacted by the General Assembly, That the taxes on
2 the persons and subjects in this chapter mentioned, or required by
3 law to be listed or assessed, shall be yearly as follows:

Taxes on lands and lots.

4   On tracts of lands and lots, with the improvements thereon, not
5 exempt from taxation, *forty cents* on every hundred dollars value
6 thereof: and herein shall be included all tracts of lands and lots,
7 with improvements thereon, not otherwise taxed or exempt from
8 taxation, of incorporated joint stock companies, savings institutions
9 and insurance companies.

On personal property.

2. On all the personal property, excepting provisions and wool
2 of last year's clip, but this section shall not be so construed as to
3 exclude from taxation any provisions purchased for sale by the holder

4 thereof, moneys and credits. as defined in this section, including all
5 capital, personal property and moneys of incorporated joint stock
6 companies (other than railroad, canal or turnpike companies), and
7 all capital invested, used or employed in any manufacturing, trade
8 or other business, forty cents on every hundred dollars value thereof.
9 But slaves and property otherwise taxed, and property from which
10 any income so taxed is derived, or on the capital invested in any
11 trade or business, in respect to which a license so taxed is issued,
12 certificates of stock, moneys and personal property that constitute
13 part of the capital of any bank, savings institutions and insurance
14 companies, whether incorporated by this or any other state, which
15 have declared dividends within one year preceding the first day of
16 February, of as much as six per cent. profits, shall not be taxed
17 under the provisions of this section. The word "moneys" shall be
18 construed to include not only gold, silver and copper coins, but bul-
19 lion and bank notes. The word "credits" shall be construed to
20 mean all bank, state or corporation stocks, claims or demands owing
21 or coming to any person, whether due or not, and whether payable
22 in money or other thing. Moneys and credits owned by any resident
23 of this state, whether such moneys or credits are within or without
24 this state, shall be taxed at the rate prescribed by this section.

On slaves.

3. On every slave who has attained the age of twelve years,
2 whether owned or hired, or whether exempted from county levy in
3 consequence of bodily infirmity or not, one dollar and twenty cents;

4 and no company exempted by its charter from taxation, shall be
5 entitled to any such exemption from taxation of any slave acquired
6 since the adoption of the constitution, or by any law exempting the
7 property of railroad or canal companies, upon the payment of taxes
8 on freight or passengers.

On free negroes.

4. On every male free negro who has attained the age of twenty-
2 one years, eighty cents; but no tax shall hereafter be assessed or
3 collected on such male free negro under the act of the 6th of April,
4 1853, establishing a colonization board.

On white males.

5. On every white male inhabitant who has attained the age of
2 twenty-one years, not exempted from taxation by order of court in
3 consequence of bodily infirmity, eighty cents.

On public bonds.

6. On the interest or profit which way have accrued, and is sol-
2 vent, or which may have been received by any person, or converted
3 into principal so as to become an interest-bearing subject, or other-
4 wise appropriated, within the year next preceding the first day of
5 February of each year, arising from bonds and certificates of debt
6 of this or any other state or country, or any corporation created by
7 this or any other state, whether the stock of such company be
8 exempt from taxation or not, six and two-thirds per centum. But
9 such interests or profits derived from bank stock or shares of savings
10 institutions and insurance companies which pay taxes thereon into

11 the treasury, shall not be included herein, unless invested or other-
12 wise appropriated, and if so invested or otherwise appropriated, the
13 tax thereon shall be at the rate of forty cents upon every hundred
14 dollars value thereof.   If no interest shall have been received within
15 the year preceding the first day of February, then the value of
16 the principal of such bonds shall be assessed and taxed as other
17 property.

On bank dividends.

7. On the dividends declared by any bank incorporated by this
2 State, the tax shall be six and two-thirds per centum upon the
3 amount thereof, to be paid into the treasury by the bank.   If the
4 dividend be that of a bank incorporated elsewhere, the tax shall be
5 six and two-thirds per centum upon the amount thereof, to be as-
6 sessed and collected as other taxes.

On dividends of savings institutions and insurance companies.

8. On the dividends declared within the year preceding the first
2 day of February, if the same be equal to or over six per centum on
3 its capital, by savings institutions and insurance companies, to be
4 paid by such institutions and companies into the treasury respec-
5 tively, six and two-thirds per centum; but if such dividend be not
6 equal to six per centum of such capital, its capital shall be listed
7 and taxed as other property.

On income.

9. On the income, salary or fees received during the year ending
2 the first day of February of each year, in consideration of the dis-

3 charge of any office or employment in the service of the State, or
4 in consideration of the discharge of any office or employment in the
5 service of any corporation, or in the service of any company, firm
6 or person, except where the service is that of a minister of the
7 gospel, one per centum upon so much thereof as exceeds five hun-
8 dred dollars. The tax on a salary payable under this section by an
9 officer of government receiving the same out of the treasury, shall
10 be chargeable on the annual salary, on the amount drawn from the
11 treasury at the time the salary is audited and paid; and fees or
12 other income of such officer shall be listed and assessed by the com-
13 missioners as in other cases, and at the rate prescribed thereon.

On toll bridges.

10. On the yearly rent or annual value of toll bridges and fer-
2 ries other than those toll bridges and ferries exempt by their charter
3 from taxation, six per centum.

On collateral inheritances.

11. On the estate of a decedent, which passes under his will, or
2 by descent to any other person, or for any other use than to or for
3 the use of the father, mother, husband, wife, brother, sister, nephew,
4 niece or lineal descendant of such decedent, there shall be a tax of
5 two per centum of such estate.

Internal improvement companies.

12. Every rail road company or canal company shall hereafter
2 report quarterly, on the fifteenth day of March, June, September
3 and December in each year, to the auditor of public accounts, the

4 number of passengers transported and the aggregate number of

5 miles traveled by them within this commonwealth, and the gross

6 amount received by such company for the transportation of freight

7 over such road or canal, or any part thereof, or water or other im-

8 provement owned or connected therewith, during the quarter of the

9 year next preceding the first day of the month in which such report

10 is made. Such company, whose road or canal is only in part within

11 the commonwealth, shall report as aforesaid such portion only of

12 such amount received for transportation of freight, as the part of

13 the said road or canal which is within this commonwealth, bears to

14 the whole of such road or canal. If the profit of such road or canal

15 consist in whole or in part of tolls, the gross amount thereof shall,

16 for the purposes of this act, be construed to be a part of the gross

17 amount received for the transportation of freight.

       13. Such statement shall be verified by the oaths of the presi-

2 dent and the superintendent of transportation, or other proper

3 officer. Every company failing to make such report, shall be fined

4 five hundred dollars ; and any company having a subordinate board,

5 or any board managing any part of its works, may, by its by-laws,

6 create and enforce such penalties as will secure proper reports of

7 such companies. At the time of making such report, the company

8 shall pay into the treasury, for every passenger transported, a tax

9 at the rate of one mill for every mile of transportation of each of

10 such passengers, and a tax of one-half of one per centum of such

11 gross amount received for the transportation of freight and tolls.

12 Every such company paying such taxes, shall not be assessed with
13 any tax on its lands, buildings, cars, boats or other property, (other
14 than slaves,) which they are authorized by law to hold or have.
15 But if any such company fail to pay such taxes at either of the
16 terms specified therefor, then its lands, buildings, cars, boats and
17 other property shall be immediately assessed under the direction of
18 the auditor of public accounts, by any person appointed by him for
19 the purpose, at its full value, and a tax shall at once be levied
20 thereon, as on real estate and other property, at ten cents on every
21 hundred dollars' value, on account of each quarterly default, to be
22 collected by any sheriff whom the auditor may direct; and such
23 sheriff shall distrain and sell any personal property of such com-
24 pany, and pay such taxes into the treasury within three months
25 from the time when such assessment is furnished to him.

Express companies.

14. Every express company, in addition to the license tax on
2 such company, on any express business, shall make a return to the
3 auditor of public accounts, on the fifteenth day of June and Decem-
4 ber in each year, of the total receipts of such company, on account
5 of its operations within the state of Virginia, within the six months
6 preceding the first day of June and December in each year.   Such
7 returns shall be verified by the oaths of the agent and chief officers
8 of such company, at its principal office or offices in the state, in the
9 manner and according to the forms prescribed by the said auditor,
10 whether collected within or without the state.   Such express com-

11 pany shall pay on the total receipts so reported, a tax of one-half

12 of one per centum, except for the transportation of bank notes for

13 brokers and nonresidents, for which the tax shall be one-fourth of

14 one per cent. upon the amount of bank notes transported; and for

15 failure to make such report or pay such tax, a penalty of six hundred

16 dollars shall be imposed on the company so failing, to be recovered

17 as other penalties are: provided, however, that no express company,

18 through any of its agents, shall transact any business appertaining

19 to the business of a broker, unless it be for the commonwealth.

20 Such principal officer shall require from the several agents em-

21 ployed by such company a report of their transactions on oath,

22 which report, so sworn to, shall accompany the report of the chief

23 officer to the auditor of public accounts.

On suits.

15. When any original suit, attachment, (other than an attach-

2 ment sued out under the provisions of the eleventh section of chapter

3 one hundred and eighty-eight of the Code,) or other action is com-

4 menced in a circuit, county or corporation court, there shall be a

5 tax of one dollar; if it be an appeal, writ of error or supersedeas in

6 a circuit court, there shall be a tax of two dollars; if it be an appeal,

7 writ of error or supersedeas in a district court, three dollars and

8 fifty cents; and if in a court of appeals, five dollars; and all actions

9 brought in any court, whether process be issued from court in the

10 first place or not, shall be subject to said tax.

On seals.

16. When the seal of a court, of a notary public, or the seal of

2 the state is annexed to any paper, except in those cases exempted
3 by law, the taxes shall be as follows: For the seal of the state, two
4 dollars: for any other seal, one dollar and fifty cents, except in
5 cases of protests of bills or notes, the tax shall be fifty cents; and
6 herein shall be included a tax on a scroll annexed to a paper in lieu
7 of an official seal.

On wills and administrations.

17. On the probate of every will or grant of administration,
2 there shall be a tax of one dollar.

Deeds.

18. On every deed admitted to record, whether the same has
2 been recorded before or not, and on every contract relating to real
3 estate, whether it be a deed or not, which is admitted to record,
4 there shall be a tax of one dollar.

ON LICENSES.

Ordinaries.

19. The taxes on licenses shall be as follows:

2   On a license to keep an ordinary or house of public entertain-
3 ment, forty dollars; and if the yearly value of such house and
4 furniture, whether rented or kept by the proprietor, exceeds one
5 hundred dollars, and is less than two hundred dollars, the tax shall
6 be fifty dollars; and if the yearly value thereof exceeds two hun-
7 dred dollars, there shall be added to the last mentioned sum fifteen
8 per cent. on so much thereof as exceeds two hundred dollars; and
9 if the license grants the privilege of retailing ardent spirits, porter,
2

10 ale or beer, to be drank elsewhere than at such ordinary, there shall
11 be added to said license a tax of fifty dollars in addition to the
12 amount otherwise imposed; and if the business be continued, there
13 shall also be a tax of one per centum upon the amount of such sales
14 for the preceding year, in addition to the specific tax.

Private entertainments.

20. On a license to keep a house of private entertainment or a
2 private boarding house, or any other house not private, but kept for
3 public resort for any purpose, five dollars; and if the yearly value
4 of such house and furniture exceed fifty dollars, and is less than one
5 hundred dollars, the tax shall be ten dollars. If the yearly value
6 thereof exceed one hundred dollars, there shall be added to the last
7 mentioned sum ten per cent. on so much thereof as exceeds one hun-
8 dred dollars. But no house shall be deemed a private boarding
9 house with less than five boarders.

21. On every license to keep a cook shop or eating house, fifteen
2 dollars; and in addition thereto, fifteen per cent. on so much of the
3 yearly value thereof as exceeds one hundred dollars.

Bowling alleys.

22. On every license permitting a bowling alley or saloon to be
2 kept for a year, fifty dollars: provided, that where there is more
3 than one such alley kept in any one room, fifteen dollars each shall
4 be charged for the excess over one.

Billiard tables.

23. And on every license permitting a billiard table to be kept

2 for a year, one hundred dollars : provided, that where there is more

3 than one such table kept in any one room, fifty dollars each shall be

4 charged for the excess over one table : provided, that if such billiard

5 table, bowling alley or saloon, be not kept open more than four

6 months in any one year, the taxes thereon shall only be one-half of

7 these rates, but the license granted shall, at the time of granting

8 the same, be for a period of four months, or for a period of twelve

9 months.

Bagatelle tables.

24. On every license permitting a bagatelle, keno or other like

2 table to be kept for one year or any less time, twenty dollars for the

3 first, and if more than one, ten dollars for the second, and five dol-

4 lars for each additional table kept in the same house.

25. On every license to a keeper of a livery stable, one dollar

2 for each stall thereof; and herein shall be included as stalls, such

3 space as may be necessary for a horse to stand, and in which a

4 horse is or may be kept at livery otherwise than for the purpose of

5 feeding horses by one day only, and no exemption from this license

6 shall be allowed to any person in consequence of such person being

7 licensed to keep an ordinary or house of private entertainment, if

8 any horses be kept, fed or hired for compensation by the proprietor

9 thereof, except that no tax shall be required on such stalls as are

10 used for horses belonging to travelers or guests stopping at such

11 house.

26. On every license to the proprietor of a distillery, if a be-

2 ginner, the tax shall be twenty dollars; and if said distillery is to

3 be kept in operation as much as four months in the year, the tax

4 shall be thirty dollars; if for six months, forty dollars; if for nine

5 months, sixty dollars; if for a longer time than nine months, one

6 hundred dollars; and if such distillery has been kept in operation

7 as much as four months in the year next preceding the time of

8 obtaining such license, the proprietor thereof shall pay, in addition

9 to the tax imposed on beginners, one per centum on the amount of

10 sales of liquor so manufactured at such distillery for the twelve

11 months next preceding the time of obtaining such license. No com-

12 pany or firm, whether engaged in distilling grain or fruit produced

13 by themselves or not, owning a distillery, shall be exempt from taxa-

14 tion, unless the grain or fruit was the joint production of the com-

15 pany or firm owning the distillery. If the distillery is engaged in

16 distilling grain produced by the owner thereof, or fruit whether pro-

17 duced by the owner thereof or not, and is not so engaged for more

18 than four months, no tax shall be imposed; but if so engaged for

19 more than four months, whether engaged in distilling fruit or grain

20 produced by the owner or not, the tax shall be assessed and collected

21 as in this section provided.

27. On every license to a merchant or mercantile firm, where a

2 specific tax is to be paid, sixty dollars: provided, that if the capital

3 employed by said merchant or firm be shown by affidavit, to be less

4 than five hundred dollars, the tax to be paid shall be ten dollars;

5 but this proviso shall not authorize any such person to sell wine,

6 ardent spirits, or a mixture thereof; and when the tax is in propor-
7 tion to the sales, if the taxable sales shall be under one thousand
8 and one dollars, the tax shall be twenty dollars; if one thousand
9 and one and under fifteen hundred dollars, twenty-four dollars; if
10 fifteen hundred dollars and under twenty-five hundred dollars, thirty-
11 two dollars; if twenty-five hundred dollars and under five thousand
12 dollars, forty-eight dollars; if five thousand dollars and under ten
13 thousand dollars, seventy-six dollars; if ten thousand and un-
14 der fifteen thousand dollars, ninety-six dollars; if fifteen thousand
15 dollars and under twenty thousand dollars, one hundred and twelve
16 dollars; if twenty thousand dollars and under thirty thousand dol-
17 lars, one hundred and forty dollars; if thirty thousand dollars and
18 under fifty thousand dollars, two hundred and eight dollars; and if
19 over fifty thousand dollars, ten dollars for every ten thousand dol-
20 lars excess over the said sum of fifty thousand dollars.

Merchant's permission to sell ardent spirits.

28. And in every case in which the license to a merchant or
2 mercantile firm, includes permission to sell wine, ardent spirits or a
3 mixture thereof, porter, ale or beer, by wholesale and retail, or by
4 retail only, if such merchant or firm (commencing business for the
5 first time) sell by wholesale and retail, or by wholesale only, an
6 additional tax of one hundred dollars, and if by retail only, forty
7 dollars; and if such license be to a merchant or mercantile firm, to
8 continue the privilege of selling wine, ardent spirits of or a mixture
9 thereof, porter, ale or beer, if by wholesale, or by wholesale and

10 retail, or by retail only, the tax shall be one per centum on the
11 amount of such sales for the year next preceding the time of obtain-
12 ing said license, in addition to the specific tax imposed on begin-
13 ners; but said sales shall not be estimated in ascertaining the
14 amount of a merchant's license.

Merchant tailors and others.

29. Merchant tailors, lumber merchants, dealers in coal, ice or
2 wood, shall obtain licenses as merchants, and be assessed and taxed
3 thereon as other merchants are by the preceding sections of this act,
4 and shall be subject to like penalties for conducting such business
5 without a merchant's license, except that any captain or other per-
6 son having the command or control of any vessel, shall not be re-
7 quired to take out a license to sell wood by retail from such vessel.

Commission merchants.

30. The tax on every license to a commission merchant, for-
2 warding merchant, tobacco auctioneer or ship broker, shall be forty
3 dollars each for commencing business; and if to continue such busi-
4 ness after the same has been carried on for a year, the tax on such
5 license shall be two per centum on the amount of commissions re-
6 ceived; and this tax shall be in addition to such tax as may be
7 imposed on a license to such merchant or firm, to sell any goods,
8 wares or merchandise. All goods consigned to any such commission
9 merchant, forwarding merchant or tobacco auctioneer, whether such
10 goods be agricultural productions or other articles exempted in the

11 hands of the producer or owner from taxation, shall be included as
12 subjects of taxation under the provisions of this section.

Auctioneers.

31. On every license to an auctioneer or vendue master com-
2 mencing business, twenty-five dollars; and if the place of business
3 be in a town containing a population of three thousand inhabitants,
4 thirty-two dollars; if the population exceeds three thousand, an ad-
5 ditional tax of fifteen dollars for every thousand persons above that
6 number, and at that rate for any fractional excess less than one
7 thousand; but said specific tax shall in no case exceed three hundred
8 and fifty dollars. On every license to an auctioneer who deals ex-
9 clusively in real estate, two hundred and fifty dollars, and he shall
10 have the right to sell real estate at auction or otherwise. On every
11 license to an auctioneer or vendue master, in this section mentioned,
12 to continue the business after the same has been carried on for a
13 year, one-half of one per centum on the amount of taxable sales of
14 such auctioneer or vendue master; but in no case shall the tax on
15 such sales exceed one thousand dollars: provided, the tax to be
16 paid by auctioneers for the sales of molasses and sugar, shall in no
17 case exceed five hundred dollars for such sales; but the tax on sales
18 of other articles shall not be affected by this provision. But no sale
19 shall be made at any other place than the house named in the
20 license as the place of business, or at such other place as the person
21 owning the property is authorized to sell the same; and no goods
22 shall be consigned to such auctioneer for sale, unless the owner

23 thereof has obtained a merchant's license for a period as long as
24 one whole year.

Common crier.

32. On every license to a common crier, if in a town of more
2 than one thousand inhabitants, ten dollars; but he shall not be
3 authorized to act as such in the sale of any property belonging to
4 any person, unless such owner is authorized to sell such property
5 without a license, or has obtained a license to do so.

Sample merchants.

33. On every license to sell goods by sample, card or other rep-
2 resentation, two hundred dollars.

Express companies.

34. On every license permitting an express company to operate
2 throughout the state, fifty dollars.

Patent rights.

35. On every license to sell or barter the right to manufacture
2 or use any machinery or other thing patented to any person or com-
3 pany, under the laws of the United States, ten dollars in each
4 county; and no merchant shall sell the same without the additional
5 tax prescribed by this section. But patentees who are citizens of
6 Virginia shall not be subject to the tax imposed by this section.

Quack medicines.

36. On every license to sell patent, specific or quack medicines,
2 if by retail, twenty-five dollars, and if by wholesale, fifty dollars.
3 A person having a merchant's license may sell any such medicines

4 without any additional license, unless the same be sold on commis-
5 sion; in which case the additional license and tax shall be imposed.

Book agents.

37. On every license to a person obtaining subscriptions to
2 books, maps, prints, pamphlets, or periodicals, twenty-five dollars
3 for each county.   On every license to sell, or in any manner furnish
4 the same, twenty-five dollars; if the person obtaining such license
5 has not been a resident of the state two years, the tax shall in each
6 case be two hundred dollars.   But any person who has been a resi-
7 dent of the state for two years, desiring to distribute or sell any
8 religious books, newspapers, or pamphlets, may apply to the county
9 or corporation court of each county in which he may desire to dis-
10 tribute or sell the same; and such court, upon being satisfied that
11 such person is a proper person for such duty, may grant him a
12 license, without the imposition of any tax for the privilege.

Agents for renting houses or hiring negroes.

38. On every license to a person engaged as agent for the rent-
2 ing of houses, twenty-five dollars.

39. On every license to a person engaged as agent for the hiring
2 of negroes, fifty dollars.

Stallions.

40. On every license to the owner of a jackass or stallion, for
2 services of which compensation is received, twice the amount of
3 such compensation, when the charge is for such service by the sea-
4 son; and where such services are for less than a season, then twice
3

5 what a commissioner may judge to be a reasonable charge therefor.
6 The tax, however, in no case to be less than ten dollars. Such
7 license shall authorize the performance of such services in any part
8 of the commonwealth.

Theatrical performances.

41. On every license permitting theatrical performances in a
2 public theatre or elsewhere, six dollars each week of such perform-
3 ances, notwithstanding the owner of the place of exhibition shall
4 have paid the license tax required on such theatre or rooms fitted
5 for public exhibitions.

42. On every license permitting the sale of refreshments in a
2 theatre during such performances, one hundred dollars for each
3 place of sale; and no abatement shall be made, if the privilege be
4 exercised for a period of less than one year.

43. On every license permitting the proprietor or occupier of
2 any public theatre or room fitted for public exhibitions, to use the
3 same for such purposes for a year, twenty dollars, if such room be
4 in a town of less than five thousand inhabitants: forty dollars, if in
5 a town of more than five thousand, and less than ten thousand in-
6 habitants; and sixty dollars in all other towns; but the land and
7 house in which such public shows are authorized, shall not be exempt
8 from taxation as other similar property.

44. On every license permitting any public show, exhibition or
2 performance, if in a corporate town, or within five miles thereof,
3 for each time of performance, ten dollars; if elsewhere, five dollars;

4 and for every exhibition of a circus, if within a corporate town, or
5 within five miles thereof, forty dollars; if elsewhere, twenty dollars;
6 and for every exhibition of a menagerie, if within a corporate town,
7 or five miles thereof, forty dollars; if elsewhere, twenty dollars.
8 All such shows, exhibitions and performances, whether under the
9 same canvas or not, shall be construed to require separate licenses
10 therefor, whether exhibited for compensation or not; and upon any
11 such shows, exhibitions and performances being concluded, so that
12 an additional fee for admission be charged, in lieu of a return check
13 authorizing the holder to re-enter without charge, shall be construed
14 to require an additional license therefor.

Porter, ale and beer.

45. On every license to manufacture porter, ale and beer, or
2 either, fifty dollars. On every license to sell, by retail, porter, ale
3 and beer, twenty dollars; and if the business be continued for more
4 than one year, an additional tax of one per centum on the amount
5 of sales of the previous year. But if the license be to retail to be
6 drank where sold, it shall be granted upon the certificate of the
7 county or corporation court, at the terms and in every respect
8 as certificates are granted to ordinary keepers and merchants to
9 retail ardent spirits.

Stock brokers.

46. On every license to a broker who deals exclusively in stocks,
2 five hundred dolars; and he shall thereupon have the right to sell
3 the said stocks at auction or otherwise; and any person who sells

4 stocks on commission shall be regarded as a stock broker under this
5 section.

Bank note brokers.

47. On every license to a broker, seven hundred and fifty dol-
2 lars.

Insurance companies.

48. On every license to an agent or sub-agent of any insurance
2 company not chartered by this state, twenty-five dollars in each
3 county or city in which an office or place of business is situated;
4 and in addition thereto, a tax of two per cent. on the whole amount
5 of premiums received and assessments collected by such agent or
6 sub-agent or company within the state, as prescribed by law. No
7 agent or sub-agent of any such foreign insurance company shall be
8 authorized to transact any business in any county or corporation
9 other than the county or corporation for which the license has been
10 granted.

Physicians and others.

49. On every license to a physician, surgeon or dentist, five
2 dollars each; and on every license to an attorney at law, five dol-
3 lars. If the yearly income derived from the practice of any such
4 callings or professions during the year next preceding the time of
5 obtaining such license shall exceed five hundred dollars, there shall
6 be an additional tax on the excess of one per centum; and this in-
7 come shall be included in the license tax. A license to any such
8 person shall confer on him the privilege of practicing such profes-
9 sion in any part of the commonwealth.

Daguerreian artists.

50. On every license to the owner of a daguerreian or such like
2 gallery, by whatsoever name it may be known or called, if in a city
3 or incorporated town of less than five thousand inhabitants, twenty
4 dollars; if more than five thousand inhabitants, forty dollars; if
5 elsewhere, ten dollars. And if the yearly income derived from the
6 practice of said art exceed five hundred dollars in any county, city
7 or town, an additional tax of two per centum on such excess for the
8 year next preceding the time of obtaining such license: and such
9 tax shall be imposed whether an artist perform in a gallery or not.

Horses, mules, asses and jennets.

51. On every license to sell horses, mules, asses and jennets
2 which are brought into this state for sale, ten dollars in each county;
3 and the act making general regulations concerning licenses shall be
4 so far modified that the certificate for obtaining such licenses may
5 designate the county or corporation as the place of sale; and horses
6 so brought into the state, as often as they are sold, and the princi-
7 pal object of the sale is for profit, although previously sold in this
8 state, shall subject the person so selling to the tax hereby imposed.

Horses, mules, &c. sold for profit.

52. On every license to sell for others, on commission or for
2 profit, horses, mules, asses, jennets, cattle, sheep and hogs, or either
3 of them, twenty dollars; and the sale may be made under such
4 license in any county or corporation.

Carriages, buggies and other vehicles.

53. On every license to sell carriages, buggies, barouches, gigs,
2 wagons, and such like vehicles, manufactured out of this state, fifty
3 dollars in each county or corporation.

Slaves bought for profit.

54. On every license to buy slaves on commission or for profit,
2 ten dollars in each county; and on the yearly income of such busi-
3 ness in all the counties (to be taxed but once), an additional tax of
4 two per centum on such income.

General provisions.

55. After the first day of February and until the first day of
2 July in each year, and until the delivery of the commissioners' books
3 to the sheriff or collector of any county, if the same be delivered
4 after the first day of July, it shall be lawful and the duty of every
5 commissioner of the revenue to make out tickets showing the amount
6 of taxes which will be chargeable on his books when completed,
7 against any person whom he has reasonable ground to suspect is
8 about to depart from his county before the first day of July or be-
9 fore the delivery of said books to said sheriff or collector. Upon
10 the delivery of such tickets the sheriff or collector shall be author-
11 ized to make immediate distress for the taxes therein specified, and
12 to use all the remedies for the collection of such taxes as are now
13 given, after the first day of July, upon the delivery of the commis-
14 sioners' books.

56. This act shall be construed to impose a tax on all occupa-

2 tions prohibited, unless the party exercising anything so prohibited
3 show by his affidavit that his case comes under some of the excep-
4 tions to this act, or to the 38th chapter of the Code (edition of 1860),
5 making general regulations concerning licenses.

57. No license shall be construed to grant any privilege beyond
2 the county or corporation wherein it is granted, unless it be expressly
3 authorized.

58. Every license granting authority to sell, unless the license
2 be specially authorized by law for a county or corporation, shall be
3 at some specified house or place within such county or corporation.

59. Commissioners of the revenue shall furnish or cause to be
2 furnished to every tax payer to be found within his county, the
3 forms prescribed by the 65th section of chapter 35 of the Code.
4 He shall require answers, according to said section, and with his
5 books, shall transmit said forms to the auditor of public accounts.

60. Any person continuing business, after any license obtained
2 by him shall have expired, without obtaining, on or before the day
3 his former license so expired, a license for the succeeding term, such
4 person shall be assessed with twice the amount of tax otherwise
5 imposed on such license.

61. If a commissioner shall, in his list of licenses to be furnished
2 to the auditor of public accounts, charge or extend in any case a tax
3 less than the law requires, the auditor of public accounts shall deduct
4 the amount omitted to be charged or extended, from the compensa-
5 tion of the commissioner; and to enable the auditor to make an

6 examination of such lists, the commissioner shall return to him, with
7 his return of licenses, all interrogatories which may have been pro-
8 pounded by him, under the direction of the auditor of public ac-
9 counts, and answered.

62. Any subject of taxation required to be listed under the pro-
2 visions of the thirty-fifth and thirty-eighth chapter of the Code, and
3 not specially taxed herein, shall be taxed as similar subjects; except
4 that the assessor's duties under the fifty-first section of chapter thir-
5 ty-five, shall be conformed to the ninth section of this act.

63. The value of lands and lots as ascertained by the assessment
2 made under the tenth chapter of the acts of eighteen hundred and
3 fifty-five and eighteen hundred and fifty-six, passed March tenth,
4 eighteen hundred and fifty-six, under subsequent special acts, and
5 under the thirty-fifth chapter of the Code in respect to new grants,
6 shall be permanent and not be changed, except under the provisions
7 of the said thirty-fifth chapter in case of a partition or conveyance;
8 and the auditor of public accounts, after the year eighteen hundred
9 and sixty-one, may so far change the form of the commissioners'
10 land book as to show in one column the value of lands and lots
11 exclusive of buildings.

64. That the sixty-first section of chapter thirty-eight of the
2 Code and the whole of chapter 40 (edition of eighteen hundred and
3 sixty) be, and the same is hereby repealed so far as the same is not
4 hereinbefore re-enacted.

65. This act shall be in force from its passage.

AMENDMENTS

PROPOSED BY THE

Senate Committee on Finance and Claims

TO

House bill, No. 118, *Imposing Taxes for the Support of Government.*

———

Sec. 2. Strike out all after the word "*property*" in first line, to
2 the word "*thereof*" in the third line (inclusive), and insert in lieu
3 thereof the words, "*except household* provisions, and on".

Sec. 9. After the word "*be*" in the 8th line, insert the words
2 "be deducted at the rate".

Sec. 15. Line 3, before the words "*or other action*" insert the
2 word "*ejectment*" and strike out all after the words "*five dollars*"
3 in the 7th line.

Sec. 22. Line 2, strike out the words "*provided that where*"
2 and insert in lieu thereof, the words "*but if*"

Sec. 23. Line 1, strike out "*And*". Strike out in 2d line the
2 words "provided *that where*" and insert the words "*but if*". Strike
3 out in 4th line the words "*provided* that".

4

Sec. 24. Line 1, strike out the word "*Kino*".

Insert, as an independent section, after the 24th, the following :

1   "On every license permitting a kino table for one year, ono
2 hundred dollars for the first and fifty dollars for the second, and ten
3 dollars for each additional table kept in the same house".

Sec. 25. Line 8, strike out the word "used" and insert in lieu
2 thereof, the words "*kept exclusively and used*".

Sec. 27. Line 2, strike out the words "*provided that*" and
2 insert in lieu thereof, the word "*but*" ; and after the word "*em-*
3 *ployed*" in same line, insert the words "*and to be employed for the*
4 *year, including as capital the cash so used, whether borrowed or not,*
5 *and goods purchased on credit*". Line 4, strike out the words
6 "*this proviso shall not*", and insert in lieu thereof, the words "*no-*
7 *thing contained in this section shall be construed to*".

After the 31st section insert as an independent section the following:

1   "On every license to an auctioneer dealing in negroes, one thou-
2 sand dollars."

Sec. 35. Line 4th, strike out the words "*the additional*" and
2 insert in lieu thereof the words, "an additional license and the pay-
3 ment of the".

Sec. 44. Line 2, after the word "performance" insert the words,
2 "*Other than the drama, whether in a theatre or other licensed house*
3 *or not*".

Sec. 48. Strike out the entire section, and insert in lieu thereof the following:

"On every license to an agent or sub-agent of any insurance
2 company not chartered by this state, twenty-five dollars; and in ad-
3 dition thereto, a tax of one per cent. on the whole amount of pre-
4 miums received and assessments collected by such agent or sub-agent
5 or company within the state, as prescribed by law."

Sec. 50. Line 5, strike out "*two*" and insert "*one*".

Sec. 53. Add to the end of the section the following words:
2 "But this section shall not be so construed as to exempt persons
3 from taxation who may put together the parts of such vehicles as
4 may be manufactured out of this state".

Sec. 64. Line 1, after the word "*thirty-eight*" add the words
2 "and the one hundred and seventh section of chapter thirty-five".

Same section, line 2. For the word "*is*" wherever it occurs, in-
2 sert the word "*are*".

Add the two following as independent sections under the general
2 provisions of the bill:
3   "Merchant tailors and all other persons manufacturing any pro-
4 duction or material, the sale of which would be prohibited without a
5 license, shall only be charged so much tax on the sales as the value
6 of the materials sold would bear to the whole value of the manufac-
7 tured articles, to be ascertained upon the oath of the person as in
8 other cases."

9   "A license to manufacture porter, ale and beer, or either of

10 them, may be granted by the commissioner of the revenue, as in

11 other cases, without any previous certificate or order of the court;

12 but a license to sell the same, or any of them, shall be granted in

13 the same manner, and under the same certificates and restrictions as

14 are required and imposed for a license to sell ardent spirits."

BILL No. 125.

SENATE BILL.

———

A BILL

To legalize proceedings on Sunday in certain cases.

1. Be it enacted by the General Assembly, That any act or pro-
2 ceeding until and including the execution of the bond by the defen-
3 dant or his commitment in default thereof, authorized by the act,
4 entitled, "An act allowing bail in certain cases," passed 31st March,
5 1851, and the act amendatory thereof, passed 16th April, 1852, may
6 lawfully be done or had as well on Sunday as on any other day.

2. This act shall be in force from its passage.

SENATE BILL.

A BILL

A bill for the appointment of a public administrator in each county and corporation.

1. Be it enacted by the General Assembly, That there shall be
2 appointed in each county and corporation by the county or corpora-
3 tion court thereof, a public administrator of the county or corpora-
4 tion, who, before said court, shall give bond payable to the Common-
5 wealth with sufficient sureties, in a penalty of not less than
6 dollars, with condition for the faithful discharge by him of the duties
7 of his office, and make oath that he will faithfully perform the
8 duties of his office to the best of his skill and judgment.

2. If at any time three months elapse without there being any
2 executor or administrator of the estate of a decedent (except during
3 a contest about a decedents will or during the infancy or absence of
4 the executor) the court in which the will was admitted to record or
5 which has jurisdiction to grant administration on the decedents estate,
6 shall on the motion of any person, order the public administrator of
7 the county or corporation, to take into his possession the estate of
8 such decedents and administer the same; whereupon such public ad-

9 ministrator without taking any other oath of office or giving any
10 other bond or security than he may have before taken or given, shall
11 be the administrator or administrator *de bonis non* of the decedent
12 with his will annexed, if there be a will, and shall be thenceforth
13 entitled to all the rights and bound to perform all the duties of such
14 administrator. The court may, however, at any time afterwards,
15 revoke such order and allow any other person to qualify as executor
16 or administrator.

3. The sureties in any bond given under this act shall be entitled
2 to the relief provided for sureties in chapter 146 of the Code.

4. Suits may be prosecuted on any bond given under this act as
2 on any bond mentioned in the ninth section of chapter thirteen of
3 the Code of Virginia.

5. As often as a vacancy may occur in the office provided for in
2 the first section of this act, it shall be supplied by the court under
3 that section.

6. No estate shall be committed to the sheriff or other officer
2 under section tenth of chapter 130 of the Code, unless there be a
3 vacancy in the office provided for by the first section of this act.

7. This act shall be in force from the first day of January 1862.

BILL No. 129.

SENATE BILL.

A BILL

To amend the fourth section of chapter 14 of the Code, so as to increase the salary of the first clerk in the Treasurer's office.

1. Be it enacted by the General Assembly, That the fourth sec-
2 tion of chapter 14 of the Code of Virginia, be amended and
3 re-enacted so as to read as follows :

4   "§4. The Treasurer, the sum of two thousand dollars; the first
5 clerk in his office, thirteen hundred dollars; the second clerk, seven
6 hundred and fifty dollars; the third clerk, to be denominated clerk
7 of the banking department, eleven hundred and fifty dollars."

2. This act shall be in force from its passage.

SENATE BILL.

A BILL

To amend the third and fourth sections of an act passed March 15, 1850, to provide for the inspection of Guano and Plaster of Paris in the city of Richmond and town of Petersburg.

1. Be it enacted by the General Assembly, That the third and
2 fourth sections of the act passed March 15, 1850, entitled, "An act
3 to provide for the inspection of guano and plaster of paris in the
4 city of Richmond and town of Petersburg," be amended and re-en-
5 acted so as to read as follows:

6   "§ 3. From and after the passage of this act, it shall not be
7 lawful to sell or expose or offer for sale, any guano or ground plas-
8 ter of paris, ground beyond the limits of the State of Virginia,
9 within the limits of the city of Richmond or city of Petersburg,
10 whether the same be in barrels, bags, kegs or casks, unless the same
11 shall have been first inspected and marked by the inspectors ap-
12 pointed by virtue of this act, or some one of his deputies legally
13 appointed, under the penalty of twenty dollars for each and every
14 violation of this act, to be recovered by action of debt in the name
15 of the Commonwealth of Virginia, before any justice of the peace

16 in and for the city of Richmond or city of Petersburg, the one half

17 to the use of the informer, the other half to the use of the Literary

18 fund; and that all proceedings before said justice shall be such as

19 are now authorized by law in cases of small debts under his juris-

20 diction.

21   "§4. It shall be the duty of the inspector appointed by virtue

22 of this act, to inspect all guano and ground plaster, ground beyond

23 the limits of the State of Virginia, which may hereafter be exposed

24 or offered for sale, or sold within the limits of the city of Rich-

25 mond and city of Petersburg, whether the same be contained in bags,

26 barrels, kegs or casks, and to put proper marks on the same, denoting

27 the place of inspection and the quality and weight of guano or plas-

28 ter of paris contained in each bag, barrel, keg or cask, making

29 proper allowance for the weight of the bag, barrel, keg or cask in

30 which said guano or plaster of paris may be contained, according to

31 the best of his judgment."

    2. This act shall be in force from its passage.

SENATE BILL.

A BILL

To limit the right to make an entry or bring an action to recover lands or the possession thereof, west of the Alleghany mountains.

1. Be it enacted by the General Assembly, as follows: No per-
2 son shall make an entry on or bring an action to recover any land
3 lying west of the Alleghany mountains, but within ten years next
4 after the time at which the right to make such entry, or to bring
5 such action, shall have first accrued to himself or to some person
6 through whom he claims.

2. If at the time at which the right of any person to make an
2 entry on, or bring an action to recover, any such land shall have
3 first accrued, such person was an infant, married woman or insane,
4 then such person, or the person claiming through him, may, not-
5 withstanding the period of ten years shall have expired, make an
6 entry on, or bring an action to recover such land, within seven years
7 next after the time at which the person to whom such right shall
8 have first accrued, as aforesaid, shall have ceased to be under such
9 disability as existed when the same so accrued, or shall have died,
10 whichever shall first have happened.

3. ·No person shall make such entry or bring such action, but
2 within twenty-five years next after the time at which such right shall
3 have first accrued to him or some person from whom he shall have
4 derived such right, although such person may have been under such
5 disability at such time, and so remained during the whole of such
6 twenty-five years, or such seven years, as aforesaid, may not have
7 expired. And if any person having been under any such disability
8 at the time at which such right first accrued to him, shall marry,
9 become insane, transfer such right or die, no time to make such
10 entry or bring such action shall be allowed, because of such new
11 disability, or any disability of any person who shall have derived
12 such right from such person to whom the same first accrued.

4. Nothing herein shall affect any action now pending, or pre-
2 vent the making of any such entry, or bringing of any such action
3 within two years next after the passage hereof; but every such action
4 now pending, and every such entry or action that may hereafter be
5 made or brought within the last mentioned time, shall be governed
6 by the law existing immediately before the passage hereof. Nothing
7 in the nineteenth section of the one hundred and forty-ninth chapter
8 of the Code of Virginia shall allow or prevent any such entry or
9 action to, or from being made or brought, after the expiration of the
10 said last mentioned time, which by the provisions hereof shall be
11 allowed or prevented.

5. This act shall be in force from its passage.

A BILL

To amend the twenty-third section of the 61st chapter of the Code, entitled, "Of Works of internal Improvement."

1. Be it enacted by the General Assembly, That section twenty-
2 three of chapter sixty-one of the Code, is hereby amended and re-
3 enacted so as to read as follows:

4   "§23. A collector of tolls for any company may refuse to let
5 any person or thing pass on the company's work until the toll be
6 paid. [And such collector or other authorized officer of the com-
7 pany may examine upon oath or affirmation any person having charge
8 of any vessel, merchandize or thing subject to tolls or compensation
9 for the purpose of ascertaining the quantity or amount thereof; for
10 which purpose such collector or other officer may administer an oath
11 or affirmation; and any person answering falsely upon such examina-
12 tion shall be liable to prosecution and punishment for perjury as
13 provided by law.] If any person or thing pass the toll-gate or other
14 place for payment without paying or tendering the toll, such person,
15 or the owner or person in possession of such thing, shall forfeit to
16 the company ten dollars. And the like forfeiture shall be incurred

17 where any person or thing subject to the toll of a turnpike company
18 is passed through any private gate, bars or fence, for the purpose of
19 evading the payment of the toll.   Any such collector knowing of a
20 violation of this section, shall immediately make it known to the
21 president or one of the directors.   If he fail so to do, he shall for-
22 feit to the company twenty dollars; which may, if so much of his
23 compensation remain unpaid, be deducted therefrom."

    2. This act shall be in force from its passage.

BILL No. 142.

SENATE BILL.

___

A BILL

For the relief of the Orange and Alexandria railroad company.

1. Be it enacted by the General Assembly, That it shall be
2 lawful for the Orange and Alexandria railroad company to pay such
3 temporary arrearages as may be now due, or become due to the State
4 within two years next ensuing after the passage of this act, in the
5 bonds of said company, which bonds are secured by mortgage, and
6 bear interest at the rate of eight per centum per annum.

2. This act shall be in force from its passage.

BILL No. 144.

SENATE BILL.

A BILL

To incorporate the National Railroad Company.

1. Be it enacted by the General Assembly, That the directors
[2 of the Manassa gap railroad company, and such person or persons
3 as may be authorized by them, may open books of subscription at
4 such times and places as they deem expedient, and when five hun-
5 dred thousand dollars shall be subscribed, the subscribers may
6 organize a company by the election of five or more directors under
7 the name and style of the "National railroad company," under
8 which name and style they may, and they are hereby authorized and
9 empowered to construct, own and maintain a railroad from such
10 point on the Manassa gap railroad to such point on the Ohio river
11 at or near, or above, Letart Falls, as, after careful exploration and
12 survey, they may select, with such branch railways connecting their
13 main stem with the towns of Clarksburg and Parkersburg, and such
14 other towns and mines and manufactories within fifty miles of their
15 main stem, as in their discretion the said company may wish to con-

16 struct; and the subscribers may pay their subscriptions with lands
17 or with money, as may be agreed on between them and the directors
18 of the said company: and the company may take, have, possess
19 and acquire by gift, grant or purchase any property and estate, real
20 or personal, and the same may use, lease, let, mortgage, sell, transfer
21 and convey, as other owners of such property and estate may do.

   2. The said company and the Manassa gap railroad company
2 may be united and consolidated, and they are hereby authorized and
3 empowered to unite and consolidate under such name as they may
4 adopt, the terms of such union to be arranged by contract, which
5 contract shall be approved by a meeting of the shareholders; and
6 the National railroad company and the consolidated company, under
7 the name adopted as aforesaid, shall have all the rights, powers and
8 privileges which may pertain to either of them and to the Manassa
9 gap railroad company, and all such as may be necessary or proper
10 for them to have as a company organized for the purposes stated in
11 their respective acts of incorporation, and in the general and special
12 acts of Assembly in reference thereto; and may make a redistribu-
13 tion of their capital into shares, not exceeding one hundred dollars
14 each, in accordance with the actual cash value of the respective
15 shares, to be agreed upon by contract, as aforesaid: and the direc-
16 tors may from time to time increase their capital to an amount equal
17 to the cost of the construction and equipment of their said roads
18 and branches, and of the other property and estate of the company,

19 and may regulate the manner in which the shares shall be trans-
20 ferred on the books of the company.

    3. This act shall be in force from its passage, and be subject to
'2 any alteration, modification or repeal at the pleasure of the General
3 Assembly.

SENATE BILL.

A BILL

To amend the ninth section of an act passed March 24, 1848, entitled,
"An act to incorporate the Lynchburg and Tennessee railroad com-
pany."

 1. Be it enacted by the General Assembly, That the ninth sec-
2 tion of an act passed March 24, 1848, entitled, "An act to incor-
3 porate the Lynchburg and Tennessee railroad company," be, and
4 the same is hereby amended and re-enacted so as to read as follows:
5 "§9. The said common council of the town and corporation of
6 Lynchburg, shall have power and authority to assess and collect
7 taxes upon the lands, property and persons of all persons within
8 the town proper, and the corporation for half a mile about and
9 beyond its present tax-paying limits, for the foregoing purposes
10 only: provided, that the assessments so made shall be equal, and
11 that this section shall not be construed to apply to the lands, prop-
12 erty and persons of individuals residing in the county of Amherst
13 and within the said limits of half a mile."

BILL No. 149.

SENATE BILL.

———

A BILL

To enforce payment of balances due from commissioners of forfeited and delinquent lands.

1. Be it enacted by the General Assembly, That the Auditor of
2 Public Accounts shall cause to be collected, of the commissioners of
3 forfeited and delinquent lands, any balances due from them for lands
4 sold by them as such commissioners, under the orders and decrees of
5 any of the circuit courts of the counties west of the Alleghany
6 mountains.

2. And be it further enacted, That upon the failure of any such
2 commissioners to pay such balances, with the proper interest thereon,
3 into the treasury, it shall be the duty of the Auditor to cause suits
4 to be instituted in the circuit courts of the counties in which such
5 commissioners may have been appointed, against such commissioners
6 and their sureties, so in default, his or their personal representa-
7 tives, for the recovery of such balance and interest as aforesaid.
8 Said proceedings may be instituted by a motion in said court, but at
9 least thirty days' notice shall be given to the parties against whom
10 such motion shall be made, and shall be served in the manner now

11 required by law for the service of notices.   And it shall be the duty

12 of such court to cause to be ascertained, the amount for which such

13 commissioner may or may have been liable for as such commissioner,

14 together with the interest thereon, and render a judgment, in the

15 name and favor of the Commonwealth, against the parties so brought

16 before the court by such notice, which shall be collected and paid

17 into the treasury, to the credit of the Literary fund.   The proceed-

18 ings in all other respects shall be the same as in proceedings against

19 sheriffs and other officers in default to the Commonwealth; and the

20 right of appeal shall be the same.

3, This act shall be in force from its passage.

BILL No. 150.

SENATE BILL.

A BILL

To prevent abuses of the telegraph.

1. Be it enacted by the General Assembly, That any person
2 who shall wilfully transmit, or cause or procure to be transmitted,
3 by means of any telegraph line, from any place within this State,
4 to any place within or without this State, any message, despatch or
5 communication, containing any false or untrue statement, shall be
6 deemed guilty of a misdemeanor, and upon conviction thereof, shall
7 be punished by fine not exceeding five hundred dollars nor less than
8 fifty dollars, or by imprisonment in the common jail for not less
9 than ten days nor more than three months, or by both such fine and
10 imprisonment, as the court may direct.

2. Be it further enacted, That the telegraph company by whose
2 line such false or untrue statement shall be transmitted, shall be liable
3 to a penalty not less than fifty nor more than five hundred dollars:
4 provided, that if such company shall have kept a copy or record of
5 the message, despatch or communication containing the false or
6 untrue statement, together with the name of the person transmitting
7 or causing the same to be transmitted, and shall furnish and disclose

8 the same to the satisfaction of the court, it shall be lawful for the
9 court to remit such penalty.

    3. And be it further enacted, That all fines imposed by any
2 court under this act, shall be for the benefit of the informer, or, in
3 case he shall disclaim the same, for the benefit of the Literary fund;
4 and such informer, making such disclaimer, shall be a competent
5 witness in the case.

SENATE BILL.

A BILL

Authorizing a loan to the Dismal Swamp Canal company.

1. Be it enacted by the General Assembly, That it shall be law-
2 ful for the Board of Public Works, and they are hereby authorized
3 and required to loan to the Dismal Swamp canal company the sum
4 of fifty thousand dollars, to be expended in the completion of said
5 canal; the said amount to be advanced in monthly instalments of
6 eight thousand three hundred and thirty-three dollars and thirty-
7 three and one-third cents, commencing on the first day of April, one
8 thousand eight hundred and sixty-one.

2. That the Board of Public Works shall have the authority,
2 and are hereby required to raise the said sum of fifty thousand
3 dollars, in the manner and form provided by law : provided, however,
4 that no payment of money shall be made by the said Board of Public
5 Works, until the said Dismal Swamp canal company shall have exe-
6 cuted and delivered to the said board, security for the payment of
7 principal and interest of said loan, in the form of a mortgage or other
8 specific lien, to the satisfaction of said board on all net tolls, receipts
9 property, real and personal of the said company, or so much thereof and

10 as the said board may deem ample security: and provided, moreover,
11 that the said company shall, semi-annually pay into the treasury of
12 the State three and one-half per centum on the loan of fifty thou-
13 sand dollars or so much thereof as may have been paid over by said
14 Board of Public Works to said company, for the payment of the
15 interest and extinction of the principal of said loan until it shall be
16 finally discharged.

3. That in the event of default of the punctual payment of the
3 interest which shall accrue upon the loan hereby authorized; the
4 Board of Public Works are hereby empowered and directed, after
5 giving thirty days notice of such intention on their part, to take pos-
6 session of the canal and other property of said company and to hold
7 and use the same until all arrears of interest shall be paid off and
8 extinguished out of the net tolls and receipts so derived, and shall
9 then return said canal and other property to the proper authorities
10 of said company: provided, moreover, that the said Dismal Swamp
11 canal company, may at any time discharge the debt hereby created,
12 by paying into the treasury of the State any balance of principal
13 and interest then unpaid.

4. This act shall be in force from its passage.

SENATE BILL.

A BILL

To amend the forty-third section of chapter 26 of the Code.

1. Be it enacted by the General Assembly, That the forty-third
2 section of chapter 26 of the Code of Virginia, be amended and
3 re-enacted so as to read as follows :

4 "§ 43. For the further encouragement of volunteers, every offi-
5 cer and member of any volunteer corps, except merely contributing
6 and honorary members, and except also the officers and members of
7 volunteer corps in the counties of New Kent, Charles City, James
8 City, York, Warwick, Elizabeth City and the city of Williamsburg,
9 shall, during his membership, be exempt from serving upon any jury
10 except grand juries. But to guard against persons becoming mem-
11 bers of the said volunteer corps, for the purpose of avoiding serving
12 on juries, it shall be the duty of the commanding officer of every
13 company to strike from the roll of his company the name of every
14 man who fails or neglects to perform any of the duties incumbent
15 on him as a member of such company; and he shall in every such
16 case notify the court of the county, city or town in which the per-
17 son resides, that his name has been stricken from the roll, and that

18 he is liable to perform jury duty. All militia fines imposed on
19 members of volunteer companies, shall be paid into the treasuries
20 and become the property of the respective companies. They shall
21 be collected and accounted for by the sheriffs, under like penalties
22 with other militia fines."

    2. This act shall be in force from its passage.

BILL No. 166.

SENATE BILL.

A BILL

Providing for the purchase and distribution of books of instruction for the use of the military officers of the State.

1. Be it enacted by the General Assembly, That the Governor
2 be and is hereby authorized to purchase for distribution to the mili-
3 tary officers of the State, four thousand copies of the "manual of
4 instruction for the volunteers and militia of the United States,"
5 prepared under the order of the Executive, by Major Wm. Gilham,
6 instructor of tactics and commandant of cadets of the Virginia
7 Military Institute: provided, that the said work can be purchased at
8 a price not exceeding one dollar and fifty cents per copy.

2. Be it further enacted, That the sum of six thousand dollars
2 be, and the same is hereby appropriated for the purchase aforesaid,
3 to be paid out of the militia fine fund, so far as the same may be
4 sufficient, otherwise out of any money in the treasury not otherwise
5 appropriated.

3. Be it further enacted, That the books shall be so marked or
2 stamped as to designate them as the property of the State, and the
3 Adjutant General shall cause them to be distributed as follows: To
4 the commandant of each regiment of the line of volunteers and

5 battalion of volunteers, as many copies as shall be sufficient to fur-
6 nish one to each field officer, and one to the captain of each troop
7 and company for the joint use of the officers of such troop and com-
8 pany. Every officer to whom the work shall be delivered, shall give
9 a receipt for the same, binding himself to return it whenever his
10 commission shall be vacated or whenever required by the State,
11 which receipt shall be good against such officer or his estate. The
12 commandant of each regiment or battalion shall deposit the receipts
13 taken by him as herein required, in the clerk's office of the county or
14 city, and forward the clerk's receipt, together with a list of the re-
15 ceipts deposited with him, to the Adjutant General.

4. Any commandant of a regiment or battalion failing so to dis-
2 tribute and take receipts as herein directed, shall incur a fine of not
3 less than twenty dollars nor more than one hundred. And any offi-
4 cer failing to return the book or books delivered to him, shall incur
5 a fine of ten dollars, to be assessed as directed by the militia law.

5. This act shall be in force from its passage.

SENATE BILL.

———

A BILL

Amending section 6 of chapter 138 of the Code.

1. Be it enacted by the General Assembly, That section 6 of
2. chapter 138 of the Code, be amended to read as follows:
3. "§ 6. If any tenant renting for a less term than one year, from
4. whom rent is in arrear and unpaid, shall desert the demised premises,
5. and leaves the same uncultivated or unoccupied, or refuses or fails
6. to pay such rent when due, and there not being any goods thereon
7. subject to distress sufficient to satisfy the said rent, the lessor or his
8. agent may post a notice (in case of a desertion of the premises), in
9. writing, upon a conspicuous place of the premises, requiring the
10. tenant to pay the said rent within ten days; and if not paid in that
11. time, the lessor or his agent shall be entitled to possession, and may
12. enter thereon. But if the said demised premises is occupied, and
13. the tenant fails or refuses to pay the rent in arrears, in accordance
14. with the contract, and there not being any goods on the premises
15. subject to distress sufficient to pay the same, the lessor or his agent
16. may cause a notice to be served on the said tenant, requiring him to
17. appear before some justice of the peace, who shall, if he is satisfied

18 that such tenant is in arrear, and refuses payment, cause possession
19 to be delivered to the lessor or his agent, by directing any consta-
20 ble or other officer to give such possession by ejecting the said
21 occupant.

　　2. This act shall be in force from its passage.

BILL No. 170.

SENATE BILL.

A BILL

Amending the charter of Black Lick and Plaster Bank turnpike company.

1. Be it enacted by the General Assembly of Virginia, That the
2 president and directors of the Black Lick and Plaster Bank turn-
3 pike, be authorized to extend said road from some convenient point
4 on the Walkers creek and Holston turnpike, in the county of
5 Wythe, to the Tazewell courthouse, Marion and Rye valley turn-
6 pike, on Clinch mountain, in the county of Tazewell.

2. The second section of the act providing for constructing the
2 Black Lick and Plaster Bank turnpike road in Wythe and Smyth
3 counties, is hereby amended and re-enacted so as to read as follows:
4   "§ 2. The whole line of said road shall be divided by the courts
5 of directors into two divisions, the one within and through a portion
6 of the county of Wythe, as now constructed, and the other to be a
7 branch of the first, running from the plaster banks, or Chatham hill,
8 in the county of Smyth, to the Blue springs, crossing Walkers big
9 mountain, at Tilsons gap, and passing by Mount Airy depot; and
10 the directors shall compute what part of the total sum, estimated as

11 the cost of the whole road, not exceeding sixteen thousand dollars,
12 will be required for the construction of each division. The Board
13 of Public Works shall subscribe, on behalf of the State, for three-
14 fifths of the sum estimated for each or either of said divisions, when
15 said board shall be satisfied that two-fifths of the sum estimated for
16 each division has been subscribed by the court of the county within
17 which the same may lie, or by solvent individuals. Neither of said
18 counties shall be required to pay any part of the cost of said road
19 lying within the limits of the other county."

    3. Be it further enacted, That the branch road hereby author-
2 ized, shall be constructed at a width of not less than twelve feet,
3 and a grade not exceeding five degrees; and that this act shall not
4 increase the appropriation already made on the part of the State.

    4. This act shall be in force from its passage.

SENATE BILL.

A BILL

To amend the 102d and 103d sections of an act passed March 30, 1860, entitled, "An act for the assessment of taxes on persons and property.

1. Be it enacted by the General Assembly, That the 102d and
2 103d sections of an act passed March 30, 1860, entitled, "An act
3 for the assessment of taxes on persons and property," be and the
4 same are hereby amended and re-enacted, so as to read as follows:
5   "§ 102. But any person aggrieved by any entry in either
6 book, or by any assessment of a license tax, may, within one year
7 after the date of the clerk's certificate, where the entry is in either
8 book, and within one year from the assessment of said license tax,
9 apply for relief to the court in which the commissioner gave bond
10 and qualified. The attorney for the Commonwealth shall defend the
11 application, and no order made in favor of the applicant shall have
12 any validity, unless it be stated on the face thereof that such attor-
13 ney did so defend it, and that the commissioner was examined touch-
14 ing the application; provided, that any person who may have been
15 heretofore aggrieved by any entry or assessment, as aforesaid, and
16 failed to apply to the court having jurisdiction thereof, within the

17 time prescribed by law, may apply to such court within two years
18 from the passage of this act, and be relieved as if said application
19 had been made within the period aforesaid.

20   "§ 103. If the court be satisfied that the applicant is erro-
21 neously charged in such book, or so assessed with any taxes on
22 licenses, it shall certify the facts upon which it grants relief, and
23 shall order that the applicant be exonerated from the payment of
24 so much as is erroneously charged, if not already paid, and if paid,
25 that it be refunded to him: a copy of which order and certificate of
26 facts shall, within ten days after the entry thereof, be transmitted
27 by the clerk of the court to the Auditor of Public Accounts, and on
28 failure thereof, he shall forfeit double the amount so erroneously
29 charged; to be recovered on motion or by information, in the county,
30 corporation or circuit court of the county, city or town."

2. This act shall be in force from its passage.

SENATE BILL.

A BILL

Authorizing a loan to the Weston Military College.

1. Be it enacted by the General Assembly, That the board of
2 the Literary fund be, and they are hereby authorized and directed,
3 to lend, for a period of twenty years, from the capital of said fund
4 (whenever there shall be such an amount at their disposal), to the
5 Weston military college, at an interest of six per centum per annum,
6 the sum of five thousand dollars, or any less sum which the said
7 college may require: provided, that the said college shall secure to
8 the said board of the Literary fund, the repayment of the principal
9 of the sum so loaned, together with interest thereon at the rate
10 aforesaid, to be paid semi-annually, by a lien on the lands and build-
11 ings of said college; and the said board shall have the right, at any
12 time, to demand additional security, whenever, in their opinion, such
13 additional security may be deemed necessary.

2. If the said college shall fail to pay the semi-annual interest
2 which is herein provided for, it shall be the duty of said board to
3 take the necessary steps to collect the same, as often as default may
4 be made, and to collect the principal of the sum so loaned at the
5 expiration of the said twenty years.

3. This act shall be in force from its passage.

SENATE BILL.

A BILL

Authorizing the Board of Directors of the Penitentiary to make certain regulations in relation to that institution.

1. Be it enacted by the General Assembly, That the board of
2 directors of the Penitentiary be, and they are hereby authorized
3 and directed to divide ward No. 1 in said institution into two wards,
4 and to make in consequence thereof, such division of labor and work
5 in each of the wards thus made, as the said board shall direct. The
6 numbers of the remaining wards shall be changed to conform to the
7 alteration herein required.

2. Hereafter there shall be an additional assistant keeper, to be
2 denominated the eighth assistant keeper, who shall be appointed in
3 the manner prescribed for the other assistant keepers. He shall
4 perform such duties as the superintendent shall assign to him, and be
5 entitled to such compensation as is allowed to the seventh assistant
6 keeper, to be paid quarterly out of the public treasury as other
7 salaries are paid.

3. The said board of directors shall cause the cells appropria-
2 ted to the prisoners, to be heated with suitable flues in such manner
3 as to them shall seem proper, the costs of which shall be defrayed
4 by the said institution.

4. This act shall be in force from its passage.

BILL No. 188.

SENATE BILL.

A BILL

To provide temporary aid to the Penitentiary.

1. Be it enacted by the General Assembly, That the sum of
2 fifteen thousand dollars be, and the same is hereby appropriated out
3 of the treasury, to aid in the purchase of raw materials for carrying
4 on the manufacturing operations of the penitentiary—the amount to
5 be paid to the general agent in such sums as the board of directors
6 may direct. The board shall order the sums so paid, to be refunded
7 to the treasury as soon as the condition of the finances of the peni-
8 tentiary will admit.

2. This act shall be in force from its passage.

(14

SENATE BILL.

—

A BILL

To amend the seventeenth section of an act passed March 30th, 1860, for the better organization of the Militia of the Commonwealth.

1. Be it enacted by the General Assembly, That the seventeenth
2 section of the act passed March 30th, 1860, entitled, "An act for
3 the better organization of the militia of the Commonwealth," be
4 amended and re-enacted so as to read as follows:

5 "§ 17. Whenever two companies of cavalry, now or hereafter
6 organized in the same city, town, county or contiguous counties,
7 shall agree to unite, or shall be ordered by the Governor of this
8 Commonwealth to unite for such purpose, and he is hereby empow-
9 ered to give such order in his discretion, to be drilled and mustered
10 together at the same time and place, at least two days in the same
11 year, they shall constitute a squadron; and when mustered, shall be
12 commanded by the senior officer present belonging to the same."

2. This act shall be in force from its passage.

SENATE BILL.

A BILL

To amend the 29th section of chapter 58 of the Code.

1. Be it enacted by the General Assembly, That the twenty-
2 ninth section of the 58th chapter of the Code of Virginia concern-
3 ing "banks of circulation," be amended and re-enacted so as to read
4 as follows:

5   "§ 29. Of the moneys paid into the public treasury of the State,
6 one-fourth shall be deposited in the Bank of Virginia, one-fourth in
7 the Farmers bank of Virginia, one-fourth in the office of discount
8 and deposit of the Exchange Bank of Virginia at Richmond, and
9 one-fourth in the Bank of the Commonwealth. If either of the
10 said banks shall at any time refuse to redeem its bills or notes in
11 gold or silver coin, no further deposits of public money shall be
12 made therein, but such deposits shall be made in such of said banks
13 as continue to redeem their bills and notes in specie. And if neither
14 so continue, or if the treasurer shall at any time have good cause to
15 believe that injury will be sustained by the State from having its
16 money deposited in the said banks or any of them, he shall make a
17 written communication to the Governor on the subject, and there-
18 after shall keep the public money in such specie paying bank or

19 banks, or such other place as the Governor may direct, until further
20 provision be made by law.   In the interval before such provision,
21 moneys to be paid into or out of the public treasury, may be re-
22 ceived or paid on the warrant of the proper auditor, requiring the
23 treasurer to receive or pay the same without any deposit being made
24 or check drawn upon a bank as prescribed by the forty-fifth chapter."

BILL No. 197.

SENATE BILL

TO INCORPORATE

THE VIRGINIA CANAL COMPANY

AND TO

TRANSFER THE RIGHTS AND FRANCHISES

OF THE

JAMES RIVER & KANAWHA COMPANY

THERETO.

CONTENTS.

A BILL

To incorporate the Virginia canal company and to transfer the rights and franchises of the James river and Kanawha company thereto.

CHAPTER I.

OF THE INCORPORATION OF THE COMPANY.

Whereas the James river and Kanawha company, at their called
2 meeting in the month of August 1860, authorized an agreement to
3 be entered into, and which was executed by the president of said
4 company in pursuance of such authority, between himself and
5 Ernest de Bellot des Minieres, and his associates, under the firm and
6 style of Bellot des Minieres, Brothers & Co., of France, and to
7 which the Board of public works of this State gave its assent, as
8 evidenced by the signature of its president thereto; which agree-
9 ment is in the following words:
10 "An Executory Agreement, entered into this first day of Septem-
11 ber, in the year eighteen hundred and sixty, between Ernest de
12 Bellot des Minieres, for himself and his associates, under the firm
13 and style of Bellot des Minieres, Brothers and Company, of France,
14 of the one part, and Thomas H. Ellis, president of the James river

15   and Kanawha company, for and on behalf of the said company, in

16   pursuance of a resolution adopted by the stockholders of said com-

17   pany, in general meeting, on the thirtieth day of August, eighteen

18   hundred and sixty, of the other part, witnesseth:

19   "Whereas, it is a matter of the highest importance to the State

20   of Virginia, that the water line between the Chesapeake bay and

21   the Ohio river, which will open the great west and southwest and its

22   immense trade to the markets of the world by the shortest, cheapest,

23   safest and most certain route, and lead to an incalculable increase

24   of the direct foreign trade of Virginia, should be promptly com-

25   pleted, the parties of the first part desiring not only to secure to

26   themselves and their associates the profits of the line when com-

27   pleted, but to France the primary advantages of the direct trade

28   with her, which the line must establish, have proposed to purchase

29   the line from Richmond to the Ohio river, with the right and obliga-

30   tion to complete the same, and the president and directors of the

31   James river and Kanawha company, and the Board of public works

32   of Virginia, concurring in these views, and sympathizing strongly

33   with the parties of the first part, in their desire to establish direct

34   trade with France, the ancient ally of the United States, the said

35   president and directors of the James river and Kanawha company,

36   have entered into negotiation with the parties of the first part, and

37   have, with the approbation of the Board of public works, entered

38   into a provisional agreement with them, as herein set forth. And

39   since it is necessary to procure the approval of the general assembly

40 to the said agreement, therefore, subject to said approval, the said
41 James river and Kanawha company do contract and agree with the
42 said parties of the first part as follows—that is to say:

43   "1. A new company shall be formed by the name and style of
44 'The Virginia Canal Company,' with a capital stock of not less than
45 twenty, nor more than thirty-five millions of dollars, in shares of
46 one hundred dollars each; to which shall be transferred all the pro-
47 perty and franchises of the James river and Kanawha company,—the
48 stockholders in the James river and Kanawha company, other than
49 the Commonwealth of Virginia, to have one share of stock in the
50 said Virginia canal company for every two shares of stock they now
51 hold; and the State to transfer to the said Virginia canal company,
52 all her rights as a stockholder in the said James river and Kanawha
53 company, upon condition that the new company perform and fulfill
54 the terms and conditions hereinafter imposed.

55   "2. The Virginia canal company shall be organized with a char-
56 ter similar to the original charter of the James river and Kanawha
57 company, with such modifications and additions, as may be necessary
58 and proper for adapting it to the purposes of the new organization.

59   "3. The Virginia canal company shall clear out the deposits in
60 the present line from Richmond to Buchanan, and repair all the
61 present works, that is, the embankments, aqueducts, bridges, cul-
62 verts, waste weirs, locks, dams, houses and structures of every kind,
63 repairing those wanting repairs only, and building anew the works
64 requiring to be rebuilt, so that the whole line from Richmond to

65 Buchanan shall be of a depth of not less than five feet at any point,

66 and in all respects in a perfect state of repair.

67   "4. They shall keep on all the line a sufficient number of dredge

68 boats to keep the water way continually free from deposit and ob-

69 structions of every kind, and a sufficient number of extra lock gates

70 and wickets ready to be inserted in case of accident. They shall

71 likewise have weigh locks at not less than three points on the line.

72   "5. They shall complete the water line of improvement from

73 Buchanan to the Kanawha river, and the improvement of the

74 Kanawha river, so as to make a continuous water line from tide-

75 water at Richmond to the Ohio river; constructing the works on the

76 general plan of the part of the improvement that has already been

77 made, but with the following modifications, to wit:

78   "The locks from Buchanan to the Greenbrier river shall be

79 not less than one hundred and twenty feet long between the

80 gates, by twenty feet wide in the clear, and on the Greenbrier

81 and New rivers, and on the Kanawha river at and above Lykens'

82 shoals, not less than two hundred feet long between the gates,

83 by forty feet wide in the clear, and the works from Buchanan

84 to the foot of Lykens' shoals on the Kanawha river shall be so

85 constructed as to give a depth of water of not less than seven feet

86 at any point.

87   "The Kanawha river to be improved from Lyken's shoals to

88 its mouth in such manner as to secure a depth of water of not less

89 than six feet at all seasons of the year; the channel through the

90 shoals to be eighty feet wide at the bottom, and one hundred and
91 four feet wide at the top.

92   "" The capacity of the improvement from Richmond to Bu-
93 chanan shall be enlarged by increasing the depth of the water to
94 not less than seven feet at any point, and by increasing the dimen-
95 sions of all the present locks to not less than one hundred and
96 twenty feet long between the gates, by twenty feet wide in the
97 clear, or by doubling the locks, and making the new locks of the
98 dimensions aforesaid. But the increase in the dimensions or the
99 doubling of the locks, need not be made, until the locks require
100 reconstruction or the trade of the canal shall demand it.

101   "The capacity of the Tide water connection and Richmond
102 dock shall be enlarged, so as to afford adequate accommodation to
103 the trade of the line, by opening a second communication with tide
104 water by the route of the Haxall canal, or other suitable route;
105 or instead of that, enlarging or doubling the present locks between
106 the basin and the dock, as well as the present ship lock, in such
107 manner as may be necessary to obtain a proper result; and by con-
108 structing all such other works as may be necessary for enlarging
109 the capacity of the dock and Tide water connection for the pur-
110 pose aforesaid.

111   "6. The said Virginia canal company shall issue to the re-
112 spective stockholders in the James river and Kanawha company,
113 other than the state, certificates of stock at the rate of one share

                    2

114 in the new company, for every two shares held by them in the
115 James river and Kanawha company, which shall be full satisfaction
116 of all their interest in the last mentioned company; and they shall
117 pay annually to the holders of such certificates, five per centum
118 per annum on the amounts thereof, from the date of the organiza-
119 tion of the new company, until the line shall be completed to the
120 Ohio river in the manner before mentioned, and thereafter in lieu
121 of the said five per cent. shall pay them their ratable share of the
122 profits of the company.

123   "7. The stockholders in the Virginia canal company shall
124 enjoy equal rights, except as provided in the next preceding
125 section.

126   "8. The tolls on the line shall be regulated by the Board of
127 public works, or such other authority as the general assembly may
128 substitute for the control and superintendence of the public works
129 of Virginia: provided, that during the construction of the work,
130 the tolls shall not exceed two and a half cents per ton per mile,
131 nor be less than one cent per ton per mile on merchandise and
132 manufactures; shall not exceed one and a half cents per ton per
133 mile, nor be less than five mills per ton per mile on agricultural
134 products; shall not exceed one cent per ton per mile, nor be less
135 than two and a half mills per ton per mile on products of mines
136 and forests; and, after the completion of the improvement to the
137 Ohio river, shall not exceed two cents per ton per mile, nor be less
138 than five mills per ton per mile on merchandise and manufactures;

139 shall not exceed one cent per ton per mile, nor be less than two

140 and a half mills per ton per mile on agricultural products; and

141 shall not exceed five mills per ton per mile, nor be less than two

142 and a half mills per ton per mile on products of mines and forests:

143 provided, that these rates shall apply to the through rates, but the

144 tolls on the way trade may be increased one-third: and provided,

145 further, that the toll may be brought below the minimum rate on

146 any article, by the said board or other authority, with the consent

147 of the Virginia canal company.

148   "9. The board for the management of the company shall con-

149 sist of a president and seven directors, with the privilege to the

150 company to increase the number of directors to twelve; two of the

151 directors shall be appointed by the state of Virginia in such

152 manner as she may by law provide, the other directors shall be

153 appointed by the stockholders, and the president shall also bo

154 appointed by the stockholders, but his appointment shall be subject

155 to the approval of the state in such manner as she may by law

156 provide.

157   "10. The office of the new company shall be at Richmond,

158 Virginia, but a branch may be located at Paris; the dividends and

159 other dues to the American stockholders shall be paid at the office

160 in Richmond. But the dividends and dues of the other stock-

161 holders may be paid in Paris or elsewhere, at the pleasure of the

162 new company.

163   "11. A majority of the directors shall always be present to

164 constitute a board.   The proceedings of the board shall be recorded
165 in the English language, at the office in Richmond, and be at all
166 times open to the inspection of the stockholders, and the state, by
167 such officer as she may appoint.

168   "12. The said Virginia canal company shall be organized
169 within six months from the passage of the act of the legislature
170 incorporating it, and within the same time shall commence bona
171 fide the work of construction at Buchanan and on the Kanawha
172 river, and shall also within the same time commence bona fide
173 the repairs of the line between Richmond and Buchanan; and
174 shall complete the construction of the line to Covington and the
175 repairs of the line from Richmond to Buchanan, within three
176 years from the time of commencement aforesaid, and complete
177 the Kanawha improvement from Loup creek shoals to the mouth
178 of the river within four years from the time of commencement
179 aforesaid; and shall complete the entire line from Richmond to
180 the mouth of the Kanawha river, in all respects, except the en-
181 largement of the capacity of the canal from Richmond to Buch-
182 anan, within eight years from the time of commencement aforesaid,
183 and shall complete the enlargement of the capacity of the Rich-
184 mond dock and tide-water connection, as well as the enlargement
185 of the capacity of the canal from Richmond to Buchanan, by
186 deepening the canal, as herein above provided, within ten years
187 from the said time of commencement.

188   "13. The said company shall not have the power, by mort-
189 gage, deed of trust, or other contract, to create a lien upon its

190 works and property, except that hereinafter created in favor of
191 the commonwealth of Virginia, and shall not be competent to
192 sell the same without the assent of the general assembly of
193 Virginia.

194   "14. The said company shall, in consideration of the transfer
195 aforesaid by the state of Virginia of all her rights as a stock
196 holder in the James river and Kanawha company, pay into the
197 treasury of the state, semi-annually forever, the sum of sixty-
198 seven thousand five hundred dollars; and as a guarantee for the
199 faithful compliance with the stipulations of this agreement, they
200 shall deposit with the treasurer of Virginia the sum of one million
201 of dollars in the six per cent. registered stock of the common-
202 wealth of Virginia, to be held by him upon the following terms and
203 conditions, that is to say: The interest upon the said stock, while
204 on deposit, shall be paid to the said company. When the canal
205 shall have been completed to the town of Covington, and the
206 Kanawha improvement completed from Loup creek shoals to the
207 mouth of the river, if within the times prescribed, one-half of the
208 said sum shall be returned to the said company; and when the
209 entire line shall have been completed in the manner before men-
210 tioned, to the Ohio river, if within the time prescribed, the
211 other half shall be returned to the said company: provided, the
212 annuity to the state of Virginia, and the five per centum interest
213 to the private stockholders, hereinbefore provided for, shall have
214 been punctually paid; and if the same shall not have been punc-

215 tually paid, then so much of the said sum of one million of dollars
216 as may be necessary, shall be appropriated to the payment of the
217 same, and the residue returned to the said M. de Bellot des Min-
218 ieres and his associates, or to the Virginia canal company, as may
219 be proper; but if the said company shall fail to complete the con-
220 struction of the line to Covington, and the repairs of the line from
221 Richmond to Buchanan, within three years from the time of the
222 commencement herein prescribed, or shall fail to complete the
223 Kanawha improvement from Loup creek shoals to the mouth of the
224 river within four years from the time of commencement herein
225 prescribed, or shall fail to complete the entire line from Richmond
226 to the mouth of Kanawha river, in all respects, except the enlarge-
227 ment of the capacity of the canal from Richmond to Buchanan,
228 within eight years from the time of commencement herein pre-
229 scribed, or shall fail to complete the enlargement of the Richmond
230 dock and tide-water connection, as well as the deepening of the
231 canal to Buchanan, within ten years from the time of commence-
232 ment herein prescribed, the said sum of one million of dollars shall
233 be retained and paid to the commonwealth of Virginia as stipu-
234 lated damages in money for such failure; and all the work which
235 may have been done in repair and construction, as well as all the
236 rights which the said Virginia canal company shall have acquired
237 in the property and franchises of the James river and Kanawha
238 company, shall be forfeited, and revert to the latter company as at
239 present organized, which company shall be thereupon reinstated in

240 all its rights, as if this arrangement had never been made, and
241 shall have full right and authority to re-enter upon and resume the
242 control of the whole line of improvement; and for that purpose,
243 the present organization of the James river and Kanawha company
244 shall be continued: provided, however, that if the said Virginia
245 canal company shall be unable to complete the said water-line
246 improvement from Richmond to the Ohio river within eight years
247 as aforesaid, or to complete the enlargement of the Richmond dock
248 and Tide water connection, and deepening of the canal from Rich-
249 mond to Buchanan, within ten years as aforesaid, they may have
250 two years' extension of time in each case, by paying into the trea-
251 sury of the commonwealth of Virginia, for the said commonwealth,
252 before the expiration of the said period of eight years, a half
253 million of dollars, if they require the extension of time for the
254 completion of the water line as well as for the said enlargement;
255 or by so paying one hundred thousand dollars before the expiration
256 of ten years, if they require the extension of time only as to the
257 enlargement aforesaid; which said sums are agreed upon as liqui-
258 dated damages to be paid to the said commonwealth in the contin-
259 gencies aforesaid, for the loss sustained by such delay or delays in
260 the completion of the said works as herein required: provided,
261 however, that if the said Virginia canal company shall have pro-
262 ceeded in good faith to execute the said works, then the general
263 assembly may suspend the said forfeiture, and allow to the said
264 company such further time as to it may seem just and proper, to
265 complete the said works.

266   "15. The said Bellot des Minieres, Brothers and Company
267 shall pay to the commonwealth of Virginia so much of the three
268 hundred thousand dollars of state bonds appropriated by the act
269 of the general assembly of Virginia, passed March 23d, 1860, for
270 the improvement of the Kanawha river, as shall have been issued
271 and sold, and expended bona fide on the improvement, when they
272 shall become entitled to the property and revenues of the James
273 river and Kanawha company; and upon payment thereof, the said
274 commonwealth shall release the mortgage given by the said James
275 river and Kanawha company on the said Kanawha improvement
276 to secure the payment of the said bonds.

277   "16. As soon as the said M. de Bellot des Minieres and his
278 associates shall have been regularly incorporated according to the
279 laws of France and Virginia, and satisfactory authentication of
280 that fact communicated to the president of the James river and
281 Kanawha company and the Board of public works, and shall have
282 deposited with the treasurer of Virginia one million of dollars
283 in the six per cent. registered stock of the commonwealth, and
284 shall have deposited in one or more of the banks of the city of
285 Richmond, to the credit of the president and directors of the
286 James river and Kanawha company, for the purpose of paying
287 the floating debt of the company, the sum of four hundred thou-
288 sand dollars, to be applied to the payment of the said floating debt
289 as far as necessary, and the balance, if any, to be returned to
290 them; and shall also pay into the treasury of Virginia the amount

291 agreed to be paid by them under the next preceding section—then

292 the James river and Kanawha company shall by proper deeds con-

293 vey its entire property of every kind, to the said Virginia canal

294 company, subject to the charges before mentioned in favor of the

295 present private stockholders and the commonwealth of Virginia,

296 and subject to any present subsisting contracts for the use of the

297 water of the canal, and subject to all the provisions of this agree-

298 ment: And until this conveyance shall be made, the James river

299 and Kanawha company shall manage the said property, effects and

300 revenues under the existing laws, the said M. de Bellot des Min-

301 ieres and his associates furnishing all the means and money that

302 may be necessary to carry on the business of the company, com-

303 plete Bosher's dam, the Joshua falls dam, the dam at Lynchburg,

304 and the North river improvement, and keeping the canal in proper

305 repair—they receiving credit for all the revenues of the company.

306 But the president and directors of the present company shall have

307 no power or authority to charge the property of the company with

308 any debt, except for the purpose of keeping the line in proper

309 repair and working condition, and completing the dams and North

310 river improvement, as herein before mentioned.

311   "17. The said Virginia canal company may at any time dis-

312 charge itself from the annuity to the state of Virginia, by the

313 payment into the treasury of Virginia of the sum of two millions

314 two hundred and fifty thousand dollars in specie, but until the same

315 shall be paid, the annuity of one hundred and thirty-five thousand

316 dollars to the commonwealth shall be forever a charge upon the

317 whole property of the company, and the legislature may provide
318 by law in what manner the payment of the said annuity shall be
319 enforced.

320   "18. The European parties and stockholders may, as between
321 themselves, determine what their relative rights and obligations
322 shall be.

323   "19. The stockholders in the Virginia canal company shall
324 be required by their charter to hold at least one general meeting
325 every year in the city of Richmond.

326   "20. When this agreement shall be approved by the general
327 assembly and a charter shall be granted as provided in the first
328 and second sections thereof, the said agreement shall be binding
329 upon all the parties thereto without any further action on the part
330 of the stockholders or directors of the James river and Kanawha
331 company; and the said James river and Kanawha company binds
332 itself to use its best efforts to obtain at the earliest day possible,
333 the approval of this agreement and of the charter as provided for,
334 by the general assembly; and in the mean time the said agreement
335 shall be obligatory upon the said James river and Kanawha com-
336 pany, to the full extent that the said company has the legal au-
337 thority to act without the approval of the general assembly.

338   "And to prevent delay in the commencement of the works
339 herein before contracted to be executed, the said parties of the
340 first part shall be authorized to proceed forthwith in their said
341 undertakings; and if the general assembly shall fail to approve
342 the said agreement, and to grant said charter, then the James

343 river and Kanawha company binds itself to issue bonds under the

344 act of the 23d day of March, 1860, to the said parties of the first

345 part for an amount equal to the principal sum which may have

346 been expended upon its works as contemplated in this agreement,

347 and the interest thereon from the time when the same shall have

348 been expended until the repayment in bonds as aforesaid; and

349 the said James river and Kanawha company shall thereupon be

350 restored to all the rights conferred by its charter, as if this con-

351 tract had not been made, and the said contract shall thereafter be

352 null and void.

353   "In testimony whereof, the said Ernest de Bellot des Minieres,

354 acting for himself and the firm of Bellot des Minieres, Brothers

355 & Company, hath hereto subscribed his name and annexed his

356 seal, and the said Thomas H. Ellis, president of the James river

357 and Kanawha company, acting under authority as aforesaid, hath

358 subscribed his name and caused the seal of the company to be

359 affixed, the day and year first above written, at Richmond, Vir-

360 ginia.

361   E. DE BELLOT DES MINIERES. [Seal.]

362   THOMAS H. ELLIS,

363   [Corporate Seal.]   *Pres. J. R. & K. Co.*"

364   And whereas the general assembly of the commonwealth of

365 Virginia approve the objects and views of the contracting parties,

366 and are disposed to give to their contract validity and effect:

367 Therefore,

Company incorporated ; general powers ; restrictions thereon.

1. Be it enacted, that when the Board of public works shall
2 satisfied that the minimum capital of twenty millions of dollars has
3 been raised as provided for in the next chapter, then, in compliance
4 with the first article of said agreement, the persons constituting the
5 firm and style of Bellot des Minieres, Brothers & Co. and such
6 persons as they may admit into association with them, together
7 with the corporate and individual stockholders of the present James
8 river and Kanawha company (other than the commonwealth of Vir-
9 ginia), and such persons as may become subscribers to the capital
10 stock hereafter authorized, and their successors and assigns, shall
11 be and are hereby incorporated into a company by the name and
12 style of the "Virginia Canal Company;" and by that name, shall
13 have perpetual succession and a common seal, may sue and he sued,
14 plead and be impleaded, purchase and hold, sell and convey real
15 and personal property ; and shall be, to every intent and purpose
16 in law, the successors of the present James river and Kanawha com-
17 pany: provided, that the corporate powers shall not take effect
18 until the minimum stock shall be taken: provided, however, that
19 they shall hold no real estate, except that which by this act, or
20 some other act of the general assembly, may be vested in them, or
21 they may be authorized to acquire for the purpose of the improve-
22 ments which they are required to make ; and that they shall in no
23 wise deal as bankers or merchants, or in buying and selling any
24 produce or commodities whatsoever, except such as it is obviously

25 convenient and proper for them to purchase and sell in the regular
26 performance of the duties required of them by this act; and that
27 they shall not be engaged in the establishment or conduct of manu-
28 factures, further than for the supply of their own consumption and
29 that of the persons in their service, and in letting to farm or lease
30 sites for mills and other machinery, and water for their use.

2. The stockholders in general meeting shall have power to
2 make all such by-laws, rules and regulations, not inconsistent with
3 the constitution or laws of the land, as they may deem proper, for
4 the well ordering of the affairs of the company; for the protection
5 and preservation of their property, and for the maintenance of good
6 order and good police among their officers, agents, servants and
7 laborers, and among the boatmen and others who use their canal and
8 other works.

3. The said company shall not subscribe to the stock of any
2 other company, unless it be specially allowed by law; but this pro-
3 hibition shall not prevent it from receiving stocks or other property
4 in satisfaction of any judgment, order and decree, or as collateral
5 security for or in payment of any debt, or from purchasing stocks
6 or other property at any sale made for its benefit. If it so receive
7 shares of its own stock, it may either extinguish the same, or sell
8 and transfer such shares to a purchaser. While, however, it holds
9 such shares of its own stock, no vote shall be given thereon.

Works and property not to be encumbered or sold.

4. The said company shall not have the power, by mortgage,

2 deed of trust or other contract, to create a lien upon its works and
3 property, except that herein after created in favor of the common-
4 wealth of Virginia, and shall not be competent to sell the same
5 without the assent of the general assembly of Virginia : provided,
6 however, that it may sell or dispose of such surplus portions of its
7 real estate as may not be required for the operation of its works or
8 improvements.

Provision for repayment of money expended on Kanawha improvement.

5. The Kanawha river shall remain subject to all the existing
2 laws in relation thereto, and unaffected by this act, until the com-
3 pletion of the work now under contract and in progress upon said
4 river, provided such work shall not be completed before the first day
5 of January, 1863, upon payment to the commonwealth of Virginia
6 of so much of the appropriation of March twenty-third, 1860, for
7 the improvement of the Kanawha river, as shall have been bona fide
8 expended in the construction of said improvement, the said Virginia
9 canal company by the operation of this act, and the conveyance
10 herein before authorized, shall be invested with all the rights,
11 powers, franchises and privileges of the James river and Kanawha
12 company in and to said Kanawha river ; and upon payment thereof,
13 the said commonwealth shall release the mortgage given by the said
14 James river and Kanawha company on the said Kanawha improve-
15 ment to secure the payment of the said bonds ; but when the said
16 Virginia canal company shall be fully organized and vested with the
17 control of the residue of the line other than the Kanawha river, the

18 term of office of the present members of the Kanawha board shall
19 expire, and other members of said board shall be appointed—two
20 by the Virginia canal company, and three by the Board of public
21 works—all of whom shall be citizens of the state and residents of
22 the Kanawha valley : and such new Kanawha board shall have full
23 control of the Kanawha river until the payment by the Virginia
24 canal company herein before provided for, shall have been made.
25 The release aforesaid shall be drawn by the attorney general, and
26 executed by the Board of public works, as soon as satisfactory evi-
27 dence is submitted to said board of the payment aforesaid.

Transfer of works by James river and Kanawha company ; precedent
conditions.

6. When the Board of public works shall be satisfied that the
2 minimum capital, as provided in the next chapter, has been raised
3 as therein required, and the said M. de Bellot des Minieres and his
4 associates shall have deposited with the treasurer of the state of
5 Virginia, in the manner prescribed by law, one million of dollars in
6 the six per cent. registered stock of the commonwealth, and shall
7 have deposited in one or more of the banks of the city of Richmond,
8 to the credit of the president and directors of the James river and
9 Kanawha company, for the purpose of paying the floating debt of
10 that company, the sum of four hundred thousand dollars, to be
11 applied to the payment of the said floating debt as far as necessary,
12 and the balance, if any, to be returned to the said M. de Bellot des
13 Minieries and his associates, and satisfactory evidence of the per-

14 formance of said conditions shall have been furnished the Board of

15 public works, then the said James river and Kanawha company shall,

16 by proper deeds, convey its entire property, privileges and franchises

17 of every kind to the said Virginia canal company, subject to the

18 provisions and requirements of the fifth section of this chapter, and

19 to the conditions hereafter required in this act, and also to any pre-

20 sent subsisting contracts for the use of the water of the canal, or for

21 any other purpose.

Suits depending, how proceeded with.

7. All causes and matters which shall be depending and unde-

2 termined in any court in this commonwealth, in which the James

3 river and Kanawha company are or may be parties, plaintiff or de-

4 fendant, on the day when the said transfer is made, shall be proceed-

5 ed in, tried and determined as if the same had been commenced by

6 or against said Virginia canal company.

Transfer of rights of state of Virginia and release of its securities;
conditions.

8. When the Board of public works shall be satisfied that the

2 conditions prescribed in the sixth section have been fully complied

3 with, and that the minimum capital, as provided for in the next chap-

4 ter, shall have been raised as therein required, they shall transfer in

5 like manner to the said Virginia canal company, all the rights which

6 the state of Virginia has as a stockholder in the James river and

7 Kanawha company; and shall furthermore release all mortgages,

8 deeds of trust or other contracts, except the mortgage relative to

9 the Kanawha river, by which any lien has been created to the com-
10 monwealth upon the works and property of said James river and
11 Kanawha company, subject only to the incumbrances, limitations
12 and restrictions by this act imposed.

Rights of new company after transfer.

9. The company hereby incorporated, thenceforward shall be
2 entitled to all the tolls, rents and other emoluments, rights, fran-
3 chises, privileges and immunities, which are now enjoyed by the said
4 James river and Kanawha company, subject to the provisions and
5 limitations of the fifth section of this chapter. And the president
6 and directors of the new company, their officers and agents, shall
7 take possession of the property and works transferred as aforesaid,
8 for the benefit of the Virginia canal company.

Annuity to the state.

10. The said Virginia canal company shall, in consideration of
2 the transfer aforesaid, by the State of Virginia, pay into the treasury
3 of the state, in the mode prescribed by law, semi-annually forever,
4 the sum of sixty-seven thousand five hundred dollars. But the said
5 company may at any time discharge itself from the said annuity by
6 the payment into the said treasury of the sum of two millions two
7 hundred and fifty thousand dollars in specie; but untill the same
8 shall be paid, the said annuity shall be forever a charge upon the
9 whole property of the company; and the legislature may provide
10 by law in what manner the payment of the said annuity shall be en-
11 forced.

4

Sum to be paid to other stockholders.

11. The Virginia canal company shall furthermore take the said
2 property so to be transferred to them, subject to the payment, to
3 the corporate and individual stockholders mentioned in the second
4 chapter, of five per centum per annum on the amounts of the certi-
5 ficates of stock held by each respectively, to be computed from the
6 date of the organization of the said Virginia canal company, until
7 the water line hereinafter mentioned shall be completed to the Ohio
8 river, as herein prescribed; and thereafter, in lieu of the said five
9 per cent., shall pay to the said stockholders their ratable share of
10 the profits of the company. And for failure to perform this provi-
11 sion, the company may be proceeded against as provided hereafter
12 in the 7th chapter.

CHAPTER II.

Capital.

1. The capital stock of the Virginia canal company shall not be
2 less than twenty millions nor more than thirty-five millions of dol-
3 lars, to be divided into shares of one hundred dollars each, except as
4 herein after provided. The minimum capital shall be provided in
5 the following manner :

Minimum capital, of what composed, and how provided.

2. It shall consist of 52,000 shares of one hundred dollars each,
2 the estimated value of the interest of the state of Virginia in the
3 James river and Kanawha company, which shall be the property of
4 the Virginia canal company; ten thousand shares of one hundred
5 dollars each, the interest of the private stockholders; and not ex-
6 ceeding seven thousand shares of the same value on account of the
7 payments, by Bellot des Minieres, Brothers and Company, towards
8 the floating debt of the James river and Kanawha company, and
9 for money expended in the improvement of the Kanawha river,
10 which shall be the property of the said Bellot des Minieres, Brothers

11 and Company, and other stock which may be hereafter subscribed
12 for, sufficient to make up, with the foregoing, the sum of twenty mil-
13 lions of dollars.

    3. The certificates of stock now held by individuals or corpora-
2 tions, shall be delivered up by said individuals or corporations to
3 said Virginia canal company, and shall be canceled, and in lieu
4 thereof, certificates of the stock of said Virginia canal company
5 shall be issued to said individuals and corporations, at the rate of
6 one share for every two shares held by each, at the par value of one
7 hundred dollars each. And when any such corporate or individual
8 stockholder shall hold a number of shares which cannot be divided
9 without a fractional part of a share, the said corporation or individ-
10 ual, and their successors or personal representatives, shall be entitled
11 to the same provision therefor as is hereafter made for individual
12 stockholders who have but one share of stock.

    4. In the case of individuals holding one share of said stock
2 only, the said share shall be delivered up to said Virginia canal
3 company and be canceled, and in lieu thereof, a special certificate of
4 said company shall be issued, specifying that the said individual or
5 his assigns is entitled to one-half of one share of the capital stock
6 of said company: or the said Virginia canal company may purchase
7 said half share in each case.

    5. The said several component parts of stock heretofore sub-
2 scribed for, and hereinbefore specified, being estimated to amount in
3 the aggregate to a sum not exceeding six millions nine hundred

4 thousand dollars, shall constitute a part of the said minimum capi-
5 tal. The residue thereof shall be raised by subscriptions, of which
6 the said Bellot des Minieres, Brothers and Company may take any
7 part or the whole ; and if they shall not take the whole, the presi-
8 dent and directors of the James river and Kanawha company are
9 hereby authorized to appoint commissioners at such places in France,
10 or in this state, or elsewhere, and at such times as they may deem
11 proper, for opening books therefor, and receiving subscriptions for
12 so much as shall not have been so taken, in shares of one hundred
13 dollars each ; the amount to be paid by the subscribers in instal-
14 ments, or at one time, according to the terms of subscription pre-
15 scribed by said president and directors.

6. When subscriptions, which, with the stock hereinbefore pro-
2 vided for, shall have been obtained to the amount of twenty millions
3 of dollars, and at least one-fourth of said subscriptions shall have
4 been paid to the authorized agents of the said president and direc-
5 tors, they shall certify and establish the fact to the satisfaction of
6 the Board of public works; and shall moreover satisfy said board
7 that the subscribers are solvent and able to pay the residue, or that
8 the same has been properly secured; and thereupon, the said board
9 shall declare and so enter upon their records, that the minimum
10 capital aforesaid has been provided as required by law.

Maximum capital; how provided.

7. If the said company shall deem it necessary to increase their
2 capital to the maximum amount of $35,000,000, or to any amount

3 between the minimum and maximum capital, they shall be authorized
4 to raise the amount by subscription in such manner as they may
5 deem expedient and provide by their by-laws.

How stock transferred, when stockholders refuse or fail to transfer it.

8. In case any stockholder of the said James river and Kanawha
2 company shall be incapacitated by any cause from receiving, or
3 shall refuse or fail to receive the certificate of stock to which he
4 shall be entitled, for twelve months from the passage of this act, the
5 stock standing in his name on the books of said James river and
6 Kanawha company shall be transferred by said company to the com-
7 monwealth of Virginia, as trustee for said stockholder, and the cer-
8 tificate of stock so transferred shall be delivered up by the Board of
9 public works to said Virginia canal company and be canceled, and a
10 new certificate of stock shall be issued by said Virginia canal com-
11 pany to the commonwealth of Virginia, as trustee for said stock-
12 holder, and the same shall be held by the Board of public works in
13 trust for the use and benefit of said stockholder, to be transferred
14 by said board to said stockholder, or his personal representative,
15 whenever he shall demand the same; but if it be not demanded
16 within five years from the issuing of said certificate to the common-
17 wealth, the same shall constitute a part of the Sinking fund of the
18 commonwealth of Virginia, and may be sold, and the proceeds ap-
19 plied, or the profits therefrom may be applied to the redemption of
20 the public debt: provided, that stock so held by the state shall not
21 be represented in the meetings of the stockholders of the company.

Stock ; how verified ; shares personal estate.

9. The said Virginia canal company shall keep a regular roll of
2 their stockholders, and shall furnish to each, one or more certificates
3 of his stock, as may be required, verified by the seal of the corpora-
4 tion and the signature of the president.   The stock shall be deemed
5 personal estate, and, as such, shall pass to the personal representa-
6 tive or assignee of a stockholder.

Governments not permitted to be stockholders.

10. No government of any state or country, other than the
2 government of the state of Virginia, shall become subscribers to the
3 stock of said company, nor shall any stockholder at any time assign
4 or transfer his stock to any such government; and such subscription
5 or assignment, if made, shall be void.

Transfers of stock in foreign office to be certified.

11. Any transfers of stock which may be made in the foreign
2 office hereby authorized to be opened in Paris, shall be certified by
3 the officer in charge of that office, at the end of every three months
4 to the company's office in Richmond, there to be transferred and re-
5 corded in the general transfer books of said company.

Foreigners to be subject to tribunals of Virginia only.

12. All citizens or subjects of any foreign state or country who
2 are or may be hereafter interested in the stock, property or fran-
3 chises of the Virginia canal company, shall accept and hold the same
4 subject to the distinct stipulation that all questions arising under the

5 legislation of Virginia in regard thereto, shall be submitted to the

6 exclusion and final jurisdiction of the tribunals of Virginia, expressly

7 renouncing and disclaiming all right to the intervention of the gov-

8 ernments to which they may be subject, in any manner whatever.

9 But controversies arising between persons residing out of the com-

10 monwealth of Virginia, in relation to any interests they may have

11 or claim in said company, or the property or stock thereof, shall not

12 be embraced in the provisions of this section.

CHAPTER III.

MEETINGS OF STOCKHOLDERS; VOTES IN MEETINGS; PRESIDENT AND
DIRECTORS; THEIR APPOINTMENT; GENERAL POWERS AND DUTIES;
OFFICES OF COMPANY; APPOINTMENT OF OFFICERS AND AGENTS, AND
HOW THEIR DUTIES AND COMPENSATION ARE PRESCRIBED.

General meeting of stockholders, how convened.

1. As soon as it shall be ascertained, as herein before provided,
2 that the minimum amount of capital has been raised, and after the
3 conditions precedent herein before set forth shall have been per-
4 formed, the said M. de Bellot des Minieres and his associates shall
5 give notice thereof, by publication in a newspaper in the city of
6 Richmond, for not less than two weeks, and call a general meeting
7 of the stockholders, to meet at a certain place in the city of Rich-
8 mond, not less than fourteen nor more than thirty days from the
9 first day of such publication. The stockholders, their executors,
10 administrators or assigns, shall stand incorporated from the time of
11 such meeting, unless in the said meeting it be determined otherwise.
12 If, on the day appointed for this or any general meeting, a sufficient
13 number of stockholders do not attend to constitute a general meet-
14 ing, those present may adjourn from time to time till a sufficient
15 number shall attend.

5

2. Annual meetings of the stockholders shall thereafter be held
2 on such day as they may in general meeting from time to time ap-
3 point, and at such place as shall be fixed from time to time by the
4 board of directors, of which notice shall be published for two weeks
5 in some newspaper printed in the city of Richmond; and there
6 shall be at least one general meeting every year in the said city of
7 Richmond, at such time as the by-laws of the said company shall
8 prescribe.

3. A general meeting of stockholders may be held at any time,
2 upon the call of the board of directors, or of stockholders holding
3 together one-twentieth of the capital stock, upon their giving notice
4 of the time and place for such meeting for thirty days in a news-
5 paper published in or near the place at which the last annual meet-
6 ing was held.

Meetings, how constituted; proxies, when appointed.

4. To constitute a general meeting, there must be present, either
2 in person or by proxy, a number of stockholders having a right to
3 give a majority of all the votes which could be given at a meeting
4 of all the stockholders, exclusive of the fifty-two thousand shares
5 before mentioned, or any portion thereof, while owned by the Vir-
6 ginia canal company. And where the stockholder desires to be
7 represented by proxy, such proxy must be appointed within fifteen
8 months of such general meeting. Such meeting may adjourn from
9 time to time until its business is completed.

Proceedings to be kept.

5. The proceedings of the stockholders at all general meetings
2 shall be regularly kept, be verified by the signature of the presiding
3 officer, and carefully preserved in well bound books; and the names
4 of all the stockholders present, whether in person or by proxy, shall
5 be entered on the minutes.

Votes of stockholders.

6. In any meeting of stockholders, each stockholder may, in
2 person or by proxy, give the following vote on whatever stock he
3 may hold in the same right, to wit: one vote for each share of stock
4 not exceeding twenty, and one vote for every ten shares exceeding
5 twenty.

7. When a vote is offered to be given at any meeting, upon
2 stock transferred within sixty days before such meeting, if any pres-
3 ent object to the vote, it shall not be counted, unless the stockholder
4 or his proxy has made or shall make oath that the stock on which
5 such vote is to be given, is held by such stockholder bona fide, and
6 not by virtue of a transfer made with intent to give more votes than
7 is allowed by the preceding section.

President and board of directors.

8. The board for the management of the affairs of the company
2 shall consist of a president and seven directors, with the privilege
3 to the company to increase the number of directors to twelve.

9. At the first general meeting and at each stated annual meet-

2 ing thereafter held in Richmond, the stockholders shall appoint the

3 president and all of the directors of the company, except two, who

4 shall hold their offices for one year, and thereafter until their suc-

5 cessors shall be appointed, unless sooner removed by the stock-

6 holders in general meeting. Two of the said directors shall be

7 appointed by the Board of public works of Virginia, or if said

8 board shall cease to exist, by such body as shall be authorized by

9 law to make the appointment, who shall hold their offices in like

10 manner, and be removed at any time by the appointing power. The

11 appointment of the president shall be certified to the governor of

12 the commonwealth of Virginia, for his approval. If disapproved,

13 the said stockholders in general meeting shall appoint some other

14 person to be president; and no person shall be president unless the

15 appointment be approved by the governor. Vacancies in the office

16 of president or directors shall be filled by the board of directors,

17 except the directors on the part of the state, whose vacancies shall

18 be filled as provided in the first appointment. A majority of said

19 directors shall be residents of the state of Virginia.

Duties and powers of president and directors.

10. The president and directors of the company, subject to the

2 control of the by-laws, shall be charged with the immediate care and

3 superintendence of the affairs of the company; with making and

4 executing their contracts, either by themselves or by their lawful

5 agents; with constructing and preserving their works; with the

6 custody and preservation of all the property of the company; and

7　with the control and direction of all of their agents. A majority

8　of the board shall constitute a quorum for the transaction of busi-

9　ness; and when the president is absent, the directors shall appoint

10　one of their own body president pro tempore. The proceedings of

11　the board shall be recorded in the English language, at the office in

12　Richmond, and be at all times open to the inspection of the stock-

13　holders and the state; and in the case of the latter, by such officer

14　as the general assembly, the Board of public works or the governor

15　may appoint.

Journals and records; how kept and authenticated.

11. The journal of said proceedings shall be verified by the

2　signature of the presiding officer, and preserved in well bound

3　books, wherein the names of the members present shall be always

4　entered, and the vote of each member recorded when he shall

5　require it. They shall cause regular books of accounts to be kept

6　of all the receipts and disbursements, and of all the dealings of the

7　company, and shall cause their books to be regularly balanced semi-

8　annually, on such days as the by-laws shall prescribe. All books,

9　papers, correspondence and funds in possession of any officer of the

10　company, shall at all times be subject to the inspection of the board,

11　or a committee thereof.

Company's office.

12. The office of the company shall be at Richmond, Virginia,

2　but a branch may be located at Paris in France; but the officers

3 under whose control said office and branch may be, shall be subject
4 to such rules and regulations as may be prescribed by the board.

Meetings of board of directors.

13. The board shall hold meetings at such times as they shall
2 see fit, or the president shall require.   Questions before it shall be
3 decided viva voce.   No member of the board shall vote on a ques-
4 tion in which he is personally interested otherwise than as a stock-
5 holder.   The names of those voting each way shall be taken down,
6 if desired at the time by any member.

Officers and agents of company; their compensation.

14. Subject to the direction and control of the stockholders in
2 general meeting, and the by-laws, the board shall appoint a secre-
3 tary and such other officers and agents as it may deem proper, and
4 prescribe their duties, liabilities and compensation.   They shall re-
5 quire from such of them as they may deem proper, bonds payable
6 to the company, with such conditions as the board may require, and
7 with such sureties as it may approve; and the officers shall hold
8 their places during its pleasure.   The compensation to the president
9 and directors shall be prescribed by the stockholders in general
10 meeting; and to all other officers, by the board of directors, unless
11 otherwise prescribed by the stockholders.

Remedy against delinquent stockholders.

10. If the money which any stockholder has to pay upon his
2 shares, be not paid as required by the president and directors, the
3 same, with interest thereon, may be recovered by warrant, action or

4 motion as aforesaid; or such shares may, after notice in a news-
5 paper for one month, of the time and place of sale, be sold at pub-
6 lic auction for ready money, and transferred to the purchaser.

16. Out of the proceeds of such sale there shall be paid the
2 charges, and the money which ought to have been paid upon the
3 said shares, with interest thereon. Any surplus shall be paid to the
4 delinquent or his representative.

17. If there be no sale for want of bidders, or if the sale shall
2 not produce enough to pay the charges, and the money which ought
3 to be paid, with interest, the company may recover against such
4 stockholder whatever may remain unpaid, with interest thereon, by
5 warrant, action or motion as aforesaid.

18. No stock shall be assigned on the books without the consent
2 of the company, untill all the money which has become payable
3 thereon shall have been paid; and on any assignment, the assignee
4 and assignor shall each be liable for any instalments which may
5 have accrued, or which may thereafter accrue, and may be proceed-
6 ed against in the manner before provided.

19. A person in whose name shares of stock stand on the books
2 of the said company, shall be deemed the owner thereof as it re-
3 gards the company.

·20. The European parties and stockholders may, as between
2 themselves, determine what their relative rights and obligations
3 shall be.

Regulations for transfers of stock.

21. If any such person shall, for valuable consideration, sell,
2 pledge or otherwise dispose of any of his shares of stock to anoth-
3 er, and deliver to him the certificate for such shares, with a power
4 of attorney authorizing the transfer of the same on the books, the
5 title of the former (both at law and in equity) shall vest in the lat-
6 ter, so far as may be necessary to effect the purpose of the sale,
7 pledge, or other disposition, not only as between the parties them-
8 selves, but also as against the creditors of and subsequent purcha-
9 sers from the former, subject to the provisions of the preceding
10 section.

22. The person to whom any such certificate may be issued, may
2 return the same to the office of the company, and in person, or by
3 an attorney acting under a power from him, assign on the books of
4 the company either the whole number of shares mentioned in such
5 certificate, or a less number. The certificate so returned shall be
6 canceled and filed in the company's office; and thereupon so many
7 new certificates shall be issued, and to such person or persons as may
8 be proper in the case.

Lost certificates renewed.

23. When a person to whom such a certificate is issued, alleges
2 it to have been lost, he shall file in the office of the company: 1, an
3 affidavit setting forth, as nearly as he can state the same, the time,
4 place and circumstances of the loss; 2, proof of his having adver-

5 tised the same in a newspaper once a week for two months ; and 3, a

6 bond to the company, with one or more sufficient sureties, conditioned

7 to indemnify all persons against any loss in consequence of issuing

8 a new certificate in place of the former : and thereupon the board

9 may direct such new certificate, and the same shall be issued accord-

10 ingly.

6

CHAPTER IV.

Surveys for route of lines.

1. The Virginia canal company may by its officers, agents or
2 servants, enter upon any lands for the purpose of examining the
3 same, and surveying and laying out such as may seem fit for the
4 uses of said company, to any officer or agent authorized by it; pro-
5 vided, just compensation be made for any injury done to the owner
6 or possessor of the land. But the company shall not, under the
7 authority of this section, throw open any fences or enclosures on
8 any land, or injure the property of the owner or possessor, or invade
9 the dwelling-house of any free person, or any space within sixty feet
10 thereof, without the consent of the owner.

How much real estate may be acquired.

2. The land acquired by the company along its line generally,
2 shall not exceed two hundred feet in width, except in deep cuts and
3 fillings; and then only so much more shall be acquired as may be
4 reasonably necessary therefor. The land which it may acquire for
5 buildings or for an abutment along its line generally, shall not ex-
6 ceed five acres in any one parcel; and the land which it may acquire
7 for buildings or other purposes of the company at the principal ter-

8 mini of its work, or at any place or places where basins may be

9 necessary for the accommodation of the trade, shall not exceed

10 thirty acres in any one parcel.

3. For the purpose of supplying water to the summit level of
2 the Alleghany mountain, and to the Greenbrier, New and Kanawha
3 rivers, the company may extend a canal to the Greenbrier river or
4 to Anthony's creek, and may acquire land not exceeding two hun-
5 dred feet on the line of said canal, except in deep cuts and fillings,
6 and then only so much more as may be necessary, and such other
7 lands on the line of said canal, or at the termini thereof, as they
8 may require for abutments for dams on said Greenbrier river or
9 creek, or elsewhere on said canal, or for lots or buildings not exceed-
10 ing five acres; and for reservoirs to supply said summit level, or
11 increasing the depth of water in said rivers, they may acquire any
12 lands which may be necessary for that purpose. And the said com-
13 pany may purchase the whole or any part of a tract of land, any
14 part of which tract will be covered by the water of said reservoirs,
15 and may build any dams and construct any works which may be
16 necessary for the formation of such reservoirs. But any land so
17 purchased which shall not be necessary for the convenient use and
18 maintenance of said reservoirs, shall be sold or otherwise disposed
19 of by the said company within five years after the said reservoirs
20 are completed.

4. The said company may contract with the owners thereof for
2 such lands along their line of improvement as they are authorized

3 to acquire for the purpose of said improvement; and the said com-
4 pany may also purchase from the owners such small parcels of land
5 as, being cut off from the main body of the tract, would be incon-
6 venient for the owner to hold, and burdensome for the company to
7 connect by bridges with the other lands of the owner, and such other
8 small parcels of land lying convenient to the company's line of im-
9 provement, and containing quarries of stone or marble, water proof
10 lime, coal, or other minerals which would be useful to the company
11 in constructing and repairing their works and carrying on their
12 appropriate business: provided, that no one parcel of land so to be
13 purchased shall exceed one hundred acres, and that the whole to-
14 gether shall not exceed two thousand acres.

5. For the purpose of assessing the damages to the owner from
2 the condemnation of his land for the use of the canal, or any feeder
3 of the canal, or for any abutment of a dam, or for the sites of toll
4 houses, stables or other buildings, or for reservoirs, there shall be ap-
5 pointed by the Board of public works for the line of the improve-
6 ment extending from tide water to Lynchburg, and for the line ex-
7 tending from Lynchburg to Covington, and for the line extending
8 from Covington to Loup creek shoals, and for the line extending
9 from Loup creek shoals to the Ohio river, five assessors for each of
10 said divisions, being discreet, intelligent and impartial men, neither
11 stockholders of the company nor owners of any land through which
12 the improvements of the company will pass; who or any three or
13 more of them, shall constitute a board for the assessment of such

14 damages throughout the line of the improvement on the division for

15 which they are respectively appointed. All vacancies in the board

16 of assessors shall be filled by the Board of public works. These

17 assessors shall hold their offices during the pleasure of the Board of

18 public works, and shall receive, as a compensation for their services,

19 five dollars each for every day he shall be engaged in the perfor-

20 mance of his duties, and twenty cents for every mile he shall necessa-

21 rily travel to and from the place of performing his duties, to be paid

22 by the company.

6. Before entering upon the duties of his office, each assessor

2 shall take an oath of office before some justice of the peace within

3 this commonwealth, or before the Board of public works, or some

4 member thereof; which being duly certified, shall be preserved among

5 the files of the Board of public works, and shall be to the following

6 effect: "I, A B, do solemnly swear or affirm, that I will impartially

7 and justly, to the best of my ability, perform the duties of my office

8 of assessor to the Virginia canal company: that I will well and truly,

9 according to the best of my judgment, ascertain the damages which

10 will be sustained by the proprietor from the condemnation of his

11 land for the use of the company: that in performing this duty, I

12 will take into fair consideration the quantity and quality of the land

13 to be condemed, the additional fencing which will be required thereby,

14 and all other inconveniences and damages, which in my judgment

15 will result to the proprietor from the condemnation thereof: that I

16 will combine therewith a just regard to the advantages which the

17 owner of the land will derive from the improvement for the use of
18 which his land is condemned: and that I will unite with the other
19 assessors in truly certifying our proceedings to the proper tribunal."

     7. It shall be the duty of the assessors so appointed and quali-
2 fied, whenever they shall be thereunto required on behalf of the
3 president and directors of the company, at such time as the said
4 assessors shall appoint, and without delay, to assemble on the land
5 proposed to be condemned, and after viewing the same, and hearing
6 such proper evidence as either party may offer, they shall ascertain
7 according to the best of their judgment, and in the true spirit of the
8 oath they have taken, the damages which the proprietor of the land
9 will sustain by the condemnation thereof for the use of the company,
10 regarding such proprietor as the owner of the whole fee simple in-
11 terest therein. No such proceeding, however, shall be had without
12 consent of parties, unless ten days' previous notice of the time and
13 place shall have been given to the owner of the land, or to his guar-
14 dian, if the owner be an infant, or to the committee, the owner
15 being non compos mentis, if such owner, guardian or committee, can
16 be found within the county where the land, or any part thereof, may
17 lie; or if he cannot be so found, unless such notice shall have been
18 published at least one month next preceding, in some newspaper
19 printed as convenient as may be to such land. Any one or more of
20 the assessors attending on the day appointed, may adjourn from
21 time to time until their business shall be finished.

     8. When the assessors shall have agreed upon the amount of

2 damages, they shall forthwith make a written report of their pro-

3 ceedings, under their hands and seals, in substance as followeth :

4 "We, the undersigned, assessors to the Virginia canal company, for

5 the division from   to   do hereby certify, that after due

6 notice of the day and place appointed for our meeting, we, on the

7   day of   , that being the day so appointed (or the

8 day to which we were regularly adjourned from the day so appointed),

9 met together upon the lands of C D, in the county of

10 which the company aforesaid propose to condemn for their use, and

11 after having viewed the premises, and heard such proper evidence

12 as either party offered to us, we proceeded to estimate the quantity

13 and quality of the land aforesaid, the quantity of additional fencing

14 which would probably be occasioned by its condemnation, and the

15 following, which seemed to us all the other inconveniences and dama-

16 ges which were likely to result therefrom to the proprietor of the

17 said land—that is to say: (here the particular inconveniences and

18 damages anticipated shall be plainly set down)—that we combined

19 with these considerations, as far as we could, a just regard to the

20 advantages which would be derived by the proprietor of the land

20 from the construction of the improvement, for the use of which the

21 said land is to be condemned.   That under the influence of these con-

22 siderations, we have estimated and do hereby assess the damages

23 which will be sustained by the proprietor of the said lands from the

24 condemnation thereof for the use of the company, at the sum
25 of

26   "Given under our hands and seals this   day of
27   A. B. [Seal.]
28   C. D. [Seal.]
29   E. F. [Seal.]"

30   Such report, signed and sealed by at least three of the asses-
31 sors, together with a copy of the notice of the time and place of
32 their meeting, duly verified, shall be forthwith returned by the as-
33 sessors to the superior court for that county in which the land, or the
34 greater part thereof, may lie; and unless good cause be shown
35 against the report, it shall be confirmed by the court, and recorded
36 at the first term to which it shall be returned, or as soon thereafter
37 as may be. If the assessors be unable to agree in their assessment,
38 they shall report their disagreement to the court; and if from any
39 cause they shall fail to make and return to court a report of their
40 proceedings within a reasonable time, they may be compelled by
41 mandamus or other proper process. When the assessors report their
42 disagreement to the court, or when the report of their assessment
43 shall be disaffirmed, the court may in its discretion, as often as may
44 be necessary, remand the case to the assessors for a new report, or
45 may, pro hac vice, supersede them or any of them, and appoint
46 others in their stead; and in so remanding it, may give such instruc-
47 tions on the law as may be proper.

    9. On the confirmation of any such report, and on the payment

2 or tender to the proprietor of the land of the damages so assessed,

3 or the payment of said damages into court, when, for good cause

4 shown, the court shall so have ordered it, the land viewed and

5 assessed as aforesaid shall be vested in the Virginia canal company,

6 in the same manner as if the proprietor had sold and conveyed it to

7 them.

10. While these proceedings are depending for the purpose of

2 ascertaining the damages to the proprietor for the condemnation of

3 his land, and even before they shall have been instituted, the presi-

4 dent and directors, if they think that the interest of the company

5 requires it, may by themselves, their officers, agents and servants,

6 enter upon the lands laid out by them as aforesaid, and which they

7 desire to condemn, and apply the same to the use of the company.

8 If, when they so take possession, proceedings to ascertain the dam-

9 ages as aforesaid shall be pending, it shall be their duty diligently

10 to prosecute them to a conclusion; or if none be then pending, they

11 shall without delay institute them, and diligently prosecute them to

12 a conclusion. And when the report of the assessors, ascertaining

13 the damages, shall be returned and confirmed, the court shall render

14 judgment in favor of the proprietor of the land for the amount

15 thereof, and either compel its payment into court, or award process

16 of execution for its recovery, as to them shall seem right. In the

17 mean time no order shall be made, and no injunction shall be

18 awarded, by any court or judge, to stay the proceedings of the

19 company in the prosecution of their works, unless it is manifest that

7

20 they, their officers, agents or servants, are trascending the authority

21 given them by this act, and that the interposition of the court is

22 necessary to prevent injury that cannot be adequately compensated

23 in damages.

11. If the president and directors shall have taken possession of

2 any land before the same shall have been purchased by them, or

3 condemned and paid for according to law, and shall for sixty days

4 after so taking possession, and after the board of assessors shall

5 have been appointed and qualified as herein provided, to institute

6 proceedings for its condemnation as aforesaid, it shall be lawful for

7 the proprietor of the land to make application to the assessors; and

8 upon such application it shall be the duty of the assessors, upon ten

9 days' previous notice given to the president and directors, or any of

10 them, to proceed to assess the damages to the owner from the con-

11 demnation of his land, and to report their proceedings in like man-

12 ner, in all respects, as if application had been made to them on

13 behalf of the company; and upon such report, the same proceedings

14 shall be had in court as if it had been made on the application of

15 the president and directors, save only that when such report ascer-

16 taining the damages shall be confirmed, the court shall render judg-

17 ment in favor of the proprietor for the damages so assessed and

18 double costs; and shall thereupon either compel the company to pay

19 into court the damages and costs so adjudged, or award process of

20 execution therefor, as to them shall seem right.

12. When the judgment rendered for the damages assessed and

2 costs, shall be satisfied by the payment of the money into court or
3 otherwise, the title of the land for which such damages were assessed,
4 shall be vested in the company in the same manner as if the proprie-
5 tor had sold and conveyed it to them.

13. When the superior court shall have pronounced final judg-
2 ment in any proceeding under this act, it shall be lawful for any
3 party aggrieved by such judgment, to have the same revised and
4 reversed in the court of appeals, upon writ of error or supersedeas,
5 for error apparent on the record, in like manner as other judgments
6 of the superior courts may be revised and reversed in the court of
7 appeals.

14. The judgment upon the report of the assessors shall be no
2 bar to the recovery of damages for any injury not foreseen and
3 estimated by them, and accruing after the date of their report; and
4 to recover damages for any injury arising from the condemnation of
5 his land, accruing after the date of the report, not foreseen and
6 estimated by the assessors, the proprietor of the land, his heirs and
7 assigns, shall have remedy by proceeding before the assessors and
8 the courts, in like manner as for the original assessment of damages;
9 and if there be no such assessors, by proceeding before such other
10 tribunal, and in such manner as the legislature may hereafter pro-
11 vide: and if there be no such tribunal, then by action on the case.

15. If the said Virginia canal company, in entering upon the
2 land of any person under the authority of this act, for the purpose
3 of laying out, constructing or enlarging, altering or repairing any

4 of their said works, do any wanton or willful injury to such land or
5 its appurtenances, or to the crops growing or gathered, or to any
6 other property thereon, the said company shall pay to the person so
7 injured double the amount of the damages which shall be assessed
8 by a jury in any proper action therefor.

Company may change location; proceedings thereupon.

16. Notwithstanding a company may have made a location of
2 lands for its purposes, and proceeded to ascertain the compensation
3 therefor, the company may afterwards change its location from time
4 to time, as often as it see cause; and proceedings may be had to
5 ascertain what will be a just compensation for the lands upon any
6 such new location, and the work may be constructed upon or through
7 the same, and the title to such lands obtained in like manner as if
8 it were the first location. But whenever such change of location
9 shall be made, the title to the lands condemned for the former location
10 shall revert to the original owner, his heirs or assigns; and when
11 such change of location shall be made before the work is constructed,
12 the damages sustained by such owner by the entry of the company
13 upon his lands, shall be ascertained, and the payment thereof en-
14 forced as is herein provided when the company condemns lands for
15 its works.

Wagon ways for owners of land.

17. For every person, through whose land the roads or canals
2 of the company pass, it shall provide proper wagon ways across the
3 said roads or canals, from one part of the said land to the other,

4 and keep such ways in good repair. And if the proprietor of the

5 land and the company disagree as to the proper ways, the said asses-

6 sors shall fix the same, reserving the right to either party to appeal

7 to the circuit court of the county in which the said wagon ways are

8 to be made, which shall decide thereupon, and its decision shall be

9 final.

Not to occupy streets in a town without consent.

18. The company shall not occupy with its works the streets of

2 any town, until the corporate authority of the town shall have

3 assented to such occupation, unless such assent be dispensed with by

4 special provision of law.

How work may cross or be connected with another.

19. If said company deem it necessary, in the construction of

2 their work, to cross any rail road, turnpike or canal, or any state or

3 county road, it may do so ; provided its work be so constructed as

4 not to impede the passage or transportation of persons or property

5 along the same. If said company desire that the course of any rail

6 road, turnpike, canal or state road should be altered to avoid the

7 necessity of any crossing, or of frequent crossings, or to facilitate

8 the crossing thereof, the alteration may be made in such manner as

9 may be agreed between it and the said rail road, turnpike or canal

10 company, or the Board of public works, in the case of a state road.

11 And if such construction or alteration as is allowed by this section,

12 shall cause damage to any such company, or to the owner of any

13 lands, the said company shall pay such damage. But any county

14 road may be altered by said company for the purpose aforesaid,
15 whenever it shall have made an equally convenient road in lieu
16 thereof.

How other works may cross or be connected with it.

20. If any rail road, turnpike or canal company deem it neces-
2 sary in the construction of its work to cross the works of the Vir-
3 ginia canal company, it may do so: provided, that in crossing the
4 same the navigation shall not be impeded or obstructed, nor shall
5 the constructions and tow path of the company be in any manner
6 interfered with. No such company shall interfere with the route or
7 track for the Virginia canal company's water line as heretofore de-
8 termined, without the consent of said company.

Reservation for connecting works.

21. The legislature reserves the right to provide for connecting
2 with the works of said Virginia canal company any other work of
3 internal improvement, at such point as may seem to it proper.

How company may take materials from land for their use.

22. The said company may, by its officers, agents or servants,
2 enter upon any convenient lands for the purpose of obtaining there-
3 from wood, stone, gravel or earth, to be used in constructing such
4 work, or in repairing, enlarging or altering the same. But the
5 company shall not cut down any fruit tree, or any tree preserved in
6 any field or lot for shade or ornament, or take part of any fence or
7 building; nor take any of the said things from any lot in a town.
8 Before taking any of the said things the company, unless it agree

9 therefor with those having right thereto, shall give to the tenant of

10 the freehold, or his tenant for years, at least ten days' notice in

11 writing, that at a certain time and place, to be specified in the

12 notice, application will be made to a justice to appoint commissioners

13 to ascertain what will be a just compensation for the same. At such

14 time and place the justice shall appoint three disinterested free-

15 holders as commissioners, who, after being sworn, shall view the

16 premises, and report in writing the extent to which wood, stone,

17 gravel or earth is proposed to be taken; the nature of the injury

18 which may be done in cutting, quarrying, digging or carrying away

19 the same, and what will be a just compensation therefor. The

20 notice in writing, certificate of the commissioners having been sworn,

21 and their report, shall be forthwith returned to the court of the

22 county or corporation. If good cause be shown against the report,

23 or if the commissioners cannot agree, or fail to report within a

24 reasonable time, the court may, as often as seems to it proper, ap-

25 point other commissioners, who shall act and report in the manner

26 before prescribed. If the report be confirmed, then upon the pay-

27 ment to the person entitled thereto, or into court, of the sum so

28 ascertained, the company may take and carry away the wood, stone,

29 gravel or earth, for which such compensation may have been al-

30 lowed; and though the report may not be confirmed, yet upon the

31 payment into court of the sum therein mentioned, it may proceed

32 in like manner as if the report had been confirmed, and payment

33 made of the sum thereby ascertained. Upon the coming in of a

34 new report, after such payment into court, the court, if it affirm the

35 report, shall render judgment in like manner as in cases provided

36 for by the   section. From the time of any such judgment

37 against the company, its right so to cut, quarry, dig, take or carry

38 away, shall be suspended until the said judgment shall be satisfied.

     23. It shall be the duty of commissioners appointed under the

2 preceding section, if required so to do by the tenant of the freehold

3 or his tenant for years, to enquire in the first place whether, under

4 all the circumstances of the case, it be reasonable and proper that

5 the company should be allowed to take for its uses the timber or

6 other materials which it is proposed to condemn. If the opinion of

7 the commissioners on this point be adverse to the company, they

8 shall report the same, with the reasons on which it is founded, to

9 the court to which the justice appointing them belongs; and unless

10 said report be reversed and annulled, neither the commissioners nor

11 the company shall have power to proceed further under the section

12 aforesaid. If the opinion of the commissioners on such preliminary

13 question be favorable to the company, and the tenant of the freehold

14 and his tenant for years, if there be such, acquiesce therein, they

15 shall proceed to discharge the other duties for which they were ap-

16 pointed. But if there be not such acquiescence, the commissioners

17 shall report their opinion, with their reasons therefor, to the court

18 aforesaid, and shall not proceed further in the discharge of their

19 duties, unless their report shall be confirmed; and either party may

20 appeal from the decision of the said court to the circuit court of the

21 county, in cases arising under this and the next preceding section.

Sheriff or sergeant to attend and remove force.

24. In any case in which the company may be entitled under
2 this chapter to enter upon any lands, the sheriff or sergeant, when-
3 ever required by the company, shall attend and remove force if
4 necessary.

8

CHAPTER V.

OF THE GENERAL LINE OF THE IMPROVEMENT; THE SECTIONS AND DIVISIONS OF THE WORK, AND THE MODE OF CONSTRUCTING AND REPAIRING THE SAME; OTHER WORKS NOT TO BE INTERFERED WITH; REGULATIONS FOR ENLARGEMENT; TIME FOR COMMENCING AND COMPLETING WORKS; GUARANTEES FOR COMPLIANCE.

General line of improvement.

1. The Virginia canal company are charged with the duty of
2 connecting the James river with the navigable waters of the Ohio,
3 so as to make a continuous water line from tide water at Richmond,
4 to Point Pleasant at the mouth of the Kanawha river; constructing
5 the works on the general plan of the improvement which has already
6 been made or designated for the James river and Kanawha com-
7 pany's line, with the modifications herein after prescribed: the whole
8 work to be completed and executed in a substantial, durable and
9 workmanlike manner. Their improvement shall be kept permanently
10 in good repair, free and fit for public use, according to the provi-
11 sions of this act; and the works which they shall construct, and the
12 property which they shall acquire under the authority of law, shall
13 be vested in them and their successors forever, for their own use and
14 benefit.

Divisions of work.

2. For the better designation of the line, and for ready refer-
2 ence and description, the improvement with which the company is
3 charged shall be divided into divisions or sections, as follows:

Richmond dock.

4   First—The Richmond dock and Tide water connection, extend-
5 ing from the tide water to the basin in Richmond.   The capacity of
6 the Tide water connection and Richmond dock shall be enlarged; so
7 as to afford adequate accommodation to the trade of the line, by
8 opening a second communication with tide water by the route of the
9 Haxall canal or other suitable route, to be selected by the company,
10 and the right thereto to be acquired as prescribed in the fourth
11 chapter: or, instead of that mode of improvement, by enlarging and
12 doubling the present locks between the basin and the dock, as well
13 as the present ship lock, in such manner as may be necessary; and
14 by constructing all such other works as may be necessary for en-
15 larging the capacity of the dock and Tide water connection for the
16 purpose aforesaid.

Division from Richmond to Lynchburg.

17   Second—The first division of the canal, extending from the
18 basin in Richmond to Lynchburg, including the South side connec-
19 tions, consisting of a dam and an outlet lock at Cartersville, and
20 three bridges, to wit: one at New Canton, one at Hardwicksville and
21 one at Bent Creek, and the connection on the north side of the river
22 with the improvement of the Rivanna river.

Bill No. 197.

Division from Lynchburg to Buchanan.

23   Third—The second division of the canal, extending from Lynch-
24 burg to the town of Buchanan, including the connection with the
25 North river improvement, extending from the mouth of North river
26 to the town of Lexington.

Enlargement of the works from Buchanan to Richmond.

27   The capacity of the improvement from Buchanan to Richmond
28 shall be enlarged by said company, by increasing the depth of the
29 water to not less than seven feet at any point, and by increasing the
30 dimensions of all the present locks to not less than one hundred and
31 twenty feet long between the gates, by twenty feet wide in the clear,
32 or by doubling the locks, and making the new locks of the dimen-
33 sions aforesaid. But the increase in the dimensions or the doubling
34 of the locks, need not be made, until the locks require reconstruc-
35 tion or the trade of the canal shall demand it: and the said Vir-
36 ginia canal company may, if they think proper, increase the width
37 of the canal from Richmond to Buchanan, to seventy feet at the
38 water surface, and forty-two feet at the bottom.

Division from Buchanan to Covington.

39   Fourth—The third division of the canal, extending from Bu-
40 chanan, following the valley of James and Jackson's rivers, to
41 Covington.

Division from Covington to Greenbrier bridge.

42   Fifth—The fourth division of the canal, extending from the town
43 of Covington to the Greenbrier river.

Enlarged construction of locks and works from Buchanan west.

44   The canal from Buchanan to the Greenbrier river shall be at
45 least thirty feet wide at the bottom and fifty-one feet wide at the
46 water surface, and have a depth of water of not less than seven feet
47 at any point; but the width may be increased to forty-two feet at
48 the bottom and seventy feet at the water surface, at the option of
49 the said company, and the locks between the said points shall be not
50 less than one hundred and twenty feet long between the gates, by
51 twenty feet wide in the clear.

Division from Greenbrier bridge to Loup creek shoals.

52   Sixth—The fifth division, being the Greenbrier and New rivers,
53 extending from the intersection of the canal with the Greenbrier
54 river to the foot of Loup creek shoals on the Kanawha river. The
55 improvement on this division shall be of locks and dams adapted to
56 steam boat navigation. The locks shall be not less than two hundred
57 feet long between the gates, by forty feet wide in the clear, and
58 there shall be a depth of water in the locks at all times of at least
59 seven feet, and in the pools of not less than seven feet at any point
60 along a continuous channel, at least one hundred feet wide.

61   Seventh—The sixth division, composed of the Kanawha river,
62 extending from Loup creek shoals to its mouth on the Ohio river.

Mode of improvement on Kanawha river.

3. The said company is required to improve the Kanawha river
2 from Lykens' shoals to its mouth, in such manner and upon such
3 plan as they may adopt, so as to secure a depth of water of not less

4 than six feet at intervals not exceeding ten days, at all seasons of
5 the year: the channel through the shoals to be not less than eighty
6 feet wide at the bottom, and one hundred and four feet wide at the
7 top.

Division embracing Kanawha turnpike.

4. That part of the work heretofore a part of the James river
2 and Kanawha company's work, embracing the Kanawha turnpike
3 road, extending from Covington to the mouth of the Big Sandy
4 river, with the branch thereof from Barboursville to Guayandotte,
5 shall constitute the sixth division.

Division embracing Blue Ridge turnpike and ferry.

5. That part of the same improvement, embracing the Blue
2 Ridge turnpike and ferry; the turnpike extending from the mouth
3 of the North river, over the Blue Ridge, crossing James river by a
4 ferry, and passing down the south side of the river, shall constitute
5 the seventh division.

Repairs and preservation of turnpikes.

6. The said Virginia canal company shall at all times keep
2 open and in good repair both of said roads and keep up said ferry,
3 or substitute a bridge therefor, and shall establish such toll gates
4 thereon as they may deem proper. They may also adopt by-laws
5 and regulations prescribing a system for the repair and preservation
6 thereof, and for the transaction of business connected therewith, in
7 conformity with the powers herein before granted.

Mode of improvement of canal and locks.

7. All that part of the improvement which shall consist of a
2 continuous canal and locks, shall in all its parts, except as herein
3 before prescribed in this chapter be at least fifty feet wide at top,
4 and thirty feet wide at bottom, with not less than five feet depth of
5 water at all seasons of the year; shall be provided with a conve-
6 nient tow path at least twelve feet wide, and adapted throughout its
7 whole extent to the navigation of boats of not less than 100 tons
8 burden. To avoid very great expense at difficult passes, and to
9 furnish proper accommodation to the trade on both sides of the
10 rivers to be improved as herein provided, the width may be reduced
11 at such places, and the bed of the said rivers shall occasionally be
12 used as part of the line of navigation when the refluent water from
13 the dams will admit the convenient application of horse power. The
14 canal, at its lower termination, shall continue to be connected with
15 the tide water, so as to enable the boats which usually navigate it
16 with their cargoes, at all times conveniently to pass into tide water,
17 and descend the river or return.

Repairs of works from Richmond to Buchanan.

8. The Virginia canal company shall clear out the deposits in
2 the present line from Richmond to Buchanan, and repair all the
3 present works; that is, embankments, aqueducts, bridges, culverts,
4 waste weirs, locks, dams, houses and structures of every kind, re-
5 pairing those wanting repairs only, and building anew the works

6 requiring to be built, so that the whole line from Richmond to Buch-
7 anan shall be of a depth of not less than five feet at any point, and
8 in all respects in a perfect state of repair.

Dredge boats; extra lock gates and weigh locks.

9. They shall keep on all the line a sufficient number of dredge
2 boats to keep the water way continually free from deposit and ob-
3 structions of every kind, and a sufficient number of extra lock gates
4 and wickets ready to be inserted in case of accident. They shall
5 likewise have weigh locks at not less than three points on the line.

Change of line, how obtained.

10. The line of the improvement and the proportion of canal
2 and slack water navigation shall continue according to the present
3 arrangement of the works, where they have been executed, and ac-
4 cording to the plan which has been heretofore adopted for the im-
5 provement by the James river and Kanawha company; and where
6 the bed of Jackson's river is used, and upon the Kanawha river, the
7 water of these rivers shall not be raised by dams so as to be above
8 their banks, but with the consent of the Board of public works.
9 But if the said company shall desire or find it necessary to change
10 materially the general line of their improvement, or the mode of
11 improvement on either of the divisions not now in use for transpor-
12 tation, they shall report the alteration deemed by them to be neces-
13 sary, with plans and specifications therefor, to the Board of public
14 works. If the alteration be approved by said board, after a full in-
15 vestigation of all the circumstances connected therewith, the com-

16 pany may proceed with the work, and may obtain the right of way for
17 the new line in the manner prescribed in the preceding chapter for
18 the acquisition of land and materials, upon paying all damages as-
19 sessed as prescribed. But if the Board of public works shall deem
20 the proposed alteration injurious to the interests of the state, or of
21 such a character as to prove a nuisance to the locality in which the
22 alteration is desired, they shall have authority to prohibit the same;
23 and thereafter the company shall be confined to the route now pre-
24 scribed, and to the mode of improvement heretofore selected. And
25 the circuit court of the county in which the change is proposed to
26 be made, after the decision of the Board of public works is rendered,
27 may award an injunction to prevent the said company from execu-
28 ting any work upon the alteration proposed, and not authorized as
29 aforesaid.

Not to interfere with Central rail road.

11. The company shall not, even with the consent of the Board
2 of public works, make any alteration in their location on Jackson's
3 river, at or near Clifton Forge, by which any injury may result, or
4 any change be rendered necessary in the location of the Central
5 rail road; but if any alteration be proposed, the same may be made
6 with the assent, or by agreement with the said rail road company;
7 and if the two companies cannot agree, the change desired shall be
8 reported to the general assembly, and shall not be made unless au-
9 thorized by law.

Or with Covington and Ohio rail road.

12. And in like manner, no alteration shall be made in the loca-
2 tion of the company's line on Dunlap's creek, by which any injury
3 may result or any interference be made with the location of the
4 Covington and Ohio rail road; but if any alteration be proposed,
5 and the two companies cannot agree, the change desired shall only
6 be made by authority of the general assembly as aforesaid.

Navigation not to be interrupted to make enlargement.

13. In the enlargement of the canal, increasing its depth to
2 seven feet, and extending the length of the locks as herein before
3 prescribed, the said company shall proceed in such manner as not
4 to interrupt the navigation on the line of their improvement for a
5 longer period than two months at any time, nor oftener than three
6 times in any one year. And to insure a compliance with this pro-
7 vision, they shall, before obstructing the trade on the canal for any
8 such purpose, make report to the Board of public works of their
9 readiness to make either of the alterations contemplated; and if
10 said board are satisfied that ample means have been provided for a
11 speedy execution of the work, and that the company have all the
12 necessary materials for the new locks, aqueducts, culverts, bridges,
13 and other works, prepared and ready for use on the locality where
14 wanted, and that all the excavation, embankment and walling that
15 can be done while the water is yet in the canal, has been executed,
16 and that a force adequate to accomplish the work with the expedi-
17 tion necessary for the protection of the interests of the state, has

18 been provided, then they shall authorize the same to be forthwith
19 done. And if the said company shall not complete the same so as
20 to restore the navigation, within the time specified, the said board
21 shall proceed against the said company in the circuit court of the
22 county where the proposed work lies, by motion, on ten days' notice;
23 and if the court be satisfied that the work has not been delayed by
24 unavoidable cause, they shall impose a fine upon said company of
25 not less than one hundred nor more than one thousand dollars for
26 every week's delay beyond the time specified.

Time for commencing and completing works.

14. The said Virginia canal company shall, within six months
2 from the time of their organization under this act, commence bona
3 fide their works of construction at Buchanan, proceeding westward,
4 and also on the Kanawha river (as soon as they shall obtain posses-
5 sion thereof), and the repairs of the line between Richmond and
6 Buchanan at the same time, and shall complete the construction of
7 the line to Covington, and the repairs of the line from Richmond to
8 Buchanan, within three years from the time of commencement
9 aforesaid, and complete the Kanawha improvement from Loup creek
10 shoals to the mouth of the river, within four years from the time of
11 commencement aforesaid; and shall complete the entire line from
12 Richmond to the mouth of the Kanawha river, in all respects, except
13 the enlargement of the capacity of the canal from Richmond to
14 Buchanan, within eight years from the time of commencement afore-
15 said; and shall complete the enlargement of the capacity of the

16 canal from Richmond to Buchanan, by deepening the canal, as herein

17 before provided, within ten years from the said time of commence-

18 ment.

Guarantees for compliance.

15. As a further guarantee for the faithful compliance with the

2 provisions of this act, the said Bellot des Minieres, Brothers and

3 Company shall deposit with the treasurer of this state the sum of

4 one million of dollars in the six per cent. registered stock of the

5 commonwealth, to be held by him upon the following terms and con-

6 ditions, that is to say: The interest upon the said stock while on

7 deposit shall be paid to the said Bellot des Minieres, Brothers and

8 Company. When the canal shall have been completed to the mouth

9 of Craig's creek, one-half of the said sum shall be returned to the

10 said company; and when the entire line shall have been completed,

11 in the manner before mentioned, to the Ohio river, if within the

12 time prescribed, the other half shall be returned to the said com-

13 pany: provided the annuity to the state of Virginia, and the five

14 per centum interest to the private stockholders, hereinbefore pro-

15 vided for, shall have been punctually paid; and if the same shall

16 not have been punctually paid, then so much of the said sum of one

17 million of dollars as may be necessary, shall be appropriated to the

18 payment of the same, and the residue returned to the said Bellot

19 des Minieres, Brothers and Company. But if the said company

20 shall fail to complete the construction of the line to Covington, and

21 the repairs of the line from Richmond to Buchanan, within three

22 years from the time of the commencement herein prescribed, or
23 shall fail to complete the Kanawha improvement from Loup creek
24 shoals to the mouth of the river, within four years from the time of
25 commencement, herein prescribed; or shall fail to complete the
26 entire line from Richmond to the mouth of the Kanawha river, in
27 all respects, except the enlargement of the capacity of the canal
28 from Richmond to Buchanan, within eight years from the time of
29 commencement, herein prescribed; or shall fail to complete the
30 enlargement of the Richmond dock and Tide water connection, as
31 well as the deepening of the canal to Buchanan, within ten years
32 from the time of commencement, herein prescribed, the said sum of
33 one million of dollars shall be retained and paid to the common-
34 wealth of Virginia, as stipulated damages in money for such failure;
35 and all the work which may have been done in repair and construc-
36 tion, as well as all the rights which the said Virginia canal com-
37 pany shall have acquired in the property and franchises of the
38 James river and Kanawha company, shall be vested in and revert
39 to the latter company, under the laws in force at the time this act
40 takes effect; which company shall be thereupon reinstated in all its
41 rights, and be subject to all the liabilities, as if this arrangement
42 had never been made; and shall have full right and authority to
43 re-enter upon and resume the control of the whole line of improve-
44 ment, as prescribed in this and in the tenth chapter.

James river and Kanawha company restored to its rights.

16. For the purpose specified in the preceding section, a general

2 meeting of the stockholders of the said James river and Kanawha
3 company, existing at the time this act takes effect, or their succes-
4 sors and assigns, shall be convened by the Board of public works;
5 at which meeting the company shall be organized, as heretofore pre-
6 scribed by its charter: provided, however, that if the said Virginia
7 canal company shall be unable to complete the said water line im-
8 provement from Richmond to the Ohio river, within eight years as
9 aforesaid, or to complete the enlargement of the Richmond dock
10 and Tide water connection, and deepening of the canal from Rich-
11 mond to Buchanan, within ten years as aforesaid, they may have
12 two years' extension of time in each case, by paying into the trea-
13 sury of the commonwealth of Virginia, for the said commonwealth,
14 before the expiration of the said period of eight years, a half million
15 of dollars, if they require the extension of time for the completion of
16 the water line as well as for the said enlargement; or by paying one
17 hundred thousand dollars before the expiration of ten years, if they
18 require the extension of time only as to the enlargement aforesaid;
19 which said sums shall be as liquidated damages, to be paid to the
20 said commonwealth in the contingencies aforesaid, for the loss sus-
21 tained by such delay or delays in the completion of the said works,
22 as herein required: provided, however, that if the said Virginia
23 canal company shall have proceeded in good faith to execute the
24 said works, then the general assembly may suspend the effect of the
25 provisions above set forth as to the stipulated damages aforesaid,
26 and the vesting and reverter aforesaid, and allow to the said com-
27 pany such further time as to it may seem just and proper, to com-

28 plete the said works, providing for the enforcement of the provisions
29 suspended, in case of a second failure of said company to comply
30 with the terms required by law.

Commissioner to see whether charter is observed or violated.

17. To insure a compliance with the provisions of this charter,
2 it shall be lawful for the Board of public works or the executive at
3 any time to appoint a commissioner, who shall not be a stockholder
4 nor a creditor, nor debtor of said company, whose duty it shall be
5 to examine the proceedings of the said company, and for that pur-
6 pose, the books and records of the company shall be open to his in-
7 spection, and also to examine the works authorized to be constructed
8 and repaired; and if he shall deem that any of the requirements of
9 the charter have been violated, or omitted to be complied with, he
10 shall report the same to the Board of public works or the executive,
11 who, if they deem it of sufficient importance, shall cause proceed-
12 ings to be instituted against said company by quo warranto, in the
13 circuit court of the city of Richmond: and upon complaint or oath
14 by any person navigating the said line of improvement, or any part
15 of it, to the Board of public works, that any part of said line speci-
16 fied in such complaint is so out of repair as materially to injure the
17 navigation in such part of the line, the Board of public works may
18 appoint a commissioner to examine the same, who shall report in
19 writing the condition of said line at the part specified in the com-
20 plaint. If he shall report that the complaint is not well founded,
21 and his report is approved by the board, the complainant shall pay

22 to said commissioner five dollars per day for every day he was em-
23 ployed in making and reporting upon said examination. But if he
24 shall report that it is well founded, and the report is approved by
25 the board, the company shall pay to the said commissioner the per
26 diem compensation aforesaid. And the Board of public works may,
27 upon receiving such report, direct proceedings by motion in the
28 county court of the county in which the obstruction exists, and re-
29 cover from the said company a fine or fines not exceeding $500 for
30 every week the company shall fail to make the repairs necessary;
31 and such motion may be repeated at the discretion of the Board of
32 public works, until such repairs are made.

CHAPTER VI.

OF THE ASSESSMENT AND COLLECTION OF TOLLS; AND REGULATIONS
RELATING THERETO.

Use of works on paying tolls.

1. The Virginia canal company, upon all those parts of their
2 line of improvement transferred by this act, upon which tolls have
3 heretofore been allowed and received by the James river and Ka-
4 nawha company, shall hold the same, free for the use of all persons
5 whatever, and shall be authorized to demand and receive on such
6 persons and their property, the tolls prescribed herein, in the mode
7 and within the limits hereafter provided.

2. Whenever a section of ten miles in length, not heretofore in
2 use, shall be completed, and be opened for navigation in the manner
3 prescribed by this act, upon any portion of the canal proposed to be
4 made, the same shall be free for the use of all persons and their pro-
5 perty, upon paying the lawful tolls and conforming to the rules and
6 regulations of the company.

3. In like manner, when the improvements in the navigation of
2 the rivers hereby authorized shall have been made, their navigable
3 waters shall be public highways, free for the use of all persons and
10

4 their property, upon paying the lawful tolls, and conforming to said
5 rules and regulations.

4. The said company shall hold, in like manner, the Kanawha
2 turnpike, and the Blue Ridge turnpike and ferry, free for the use of
3 all persons and their property, upon paying the lawful tolls, and
4 conforming to said rules and regulations.

5. In like manner, all bridges or ferries heretofore the property
2 of the said James river and Kanawha company, and all rights to
3 construct other bridges or to purchase other ferries, granted to said
4 company before the passage of this act, and which have not yet been
5 constructed or purchased, and which by this charter shall pass to
6 the said Virginia canal company, shall be held by them, free for the
7 use of all persons and their property, upon paying the lawful tolls,
8 and conforming to said rules and regulations.

General rates of toll.

6. The tolls on the line may be regulated by the Virginia canal
2 company, subject to the approval of the Board of public works, or
3 such other authority as the general assembly of Virginia may sub-
4 stitute for the control and superintendence of the public works of
5 Virginia, within the limits prescribed by this section. In the mean
6 time, the said Virginia canal company may prescribe such a tariff of
7 tolls as they may deem expedient: provided, that during the con-
8 struction of the work, the tolls shall not exceed two and a half cents
9 per ton per mile, nor be less than one cent per ton per mile on mer-
10 chandise and manufactures, except salt and pig iron, on which the

11 tolls shall not be more than seven and a half nor less than two and
12 a half mills per ton per mile; shall not exceed one and a half cent
13 per ton per mile, nor be less than five mills per ton per mile on agri-
14 cultural products; shall not exceed one cent per ton per mile, nor
15 be less than two mills per ton per mile on products of mines and
16 forests, except [salt and pig iron; and after the completion of the
17· improvement to the Ohio river, shall not exceed two cents per ton
18 per mile, nor be less than five mills per ton per mile on merchandise
19 and manufactures, except salt and pig iron; shall not exceed one
20 cent per ton per mile, nor be less than two and a half mills per ton
21 per mile on agricultural products; and shall not exceed five mills per
22 ton per mile, nor be less than one mill per ton per mile on products
23 of mines and forests, and on salt and pig iron: provided, that the
24 Virginia canal company may reduce the tolls on the through freight
25 below the minimums fixed in this act; but when the tolls are so
26 reduced on through freight going east, it shall apply also to freight
27 going east from any point on the Kanawha river below the mouth of
28 the Gauley river: and provided further, that the toll may be brought
29 below the minimum rate on any article, by the Virginia canal com-
30 pany, with the consent of the said board, or other authority; and
31 provided moreover, that from the time the works on the Kanawha
32 river are delivered to the Virginia canal company, the tolls on the
33 way tonnage on that river not passing on the line of the improve-
34 ment east of the Great falls, shall not exceed one cent per ton per
35 mile, nor be less than two and a half mills per ton per mile on mer-

36 chandise and manufactures, except salt and pig iron; shall 'not ex-
37 ceed one-half cent per ton per mile, nor be less than one and a
38 quarter mills per ton per mile on agricultural products; and shall
39 not exceed two and a half mills per ton per mile, nor be less than
40 one-half mill per ton per mile on products of mines and forests, and
41 on salt and pig iron.

Tolls on the Kanawha turnpike and the Blue Ridge turnpike, and on
bridges and ferries.

    7. The said Virginia canal company shall have authority to
2 demand and collect on the Kanawha turnpike and on the Blue Ridge
3 turnpike such tolls as they may assess on each section of ten miles,
4 not exceeding three cents for every animal drawing any vehicle
5 thereon, and six cents for every wheel to any such vehicle; ten cents
6 for every person on horseback; three cents for every horse or mule;
7 one cent per head for neat cattle, and five cents per score of hogs
8 or sheep.

    8. They may assess and collect, in like manner, toll upon any
2 bridge herein before transferred to them, upon which toll has here-
3 tofore been allowed, except as herein after provided, a maximum toll
4 not exceeding three cents for every animal drawing any vehicle over
5 the same, and six cents for every wheel to any such vehicle; ten
6 cents for every person on horseback; three cents for every horse or
7 mule; one cent per head of neat cattle, and ten cents for every
8 score of sheep or hogs.

Toll on boats and passengers.

    9. The said company may also demand and collect, on any part

2 of their water line, such tolls as they may asses, on boats and other

3 water craft, not exceeding five mills per mile, and on passengers

4 conveyed by any person or company for compensation, two mills per

5 mile on each passenger. But if any company or person, in order

6 to carry on a competition with any other company or person, shall

7 carry passengers without compensation, when it is their business to

8 convey passengers, such company or person shall not be exempt

9 from such toll.

Contracts for paying toll quarterly, or commuting tolls.

10. The said company may contract with citizens residing on

2 any section of their water line, or on the line of the Kanawha or

3 Blue Ridge turnpike, for the payment of their tolls quarterly in

4 advance, or by the month or year, also with mail contractors, upon

5 such terms and under such regulations as they may prescribe; or

6 they may commute the tolls with any person, taking of him a certain

7 sum annually in lieu of tolls.

Exemptions from toll.

11. The general assembly, while the said works were in posses-

2 sion of the James river and Kanawha company, having exempted

3 certain persons and things from the payment of toll at sundry places

4 on the line of improvement, the said exceptions are continued as

5 follows, to wit:

12. No toll shall hereafter be taken from persons crossing

2 Greenbrier or Gauly bridges in a public stage coach or other riding

3 carriage, other than the toll imposed by said company on such stage

4 coach or riding carriage, and the horses or other team drawing the

5 same. No toll shall be demanded of visitors at the springs, when
6 riding or passing out and in from or to the springs for exercise, ex-
7 cept for passing Greenbrier bridge.

13. The roads and bridges which have been constructed to pro-
2 vide accommodation for the trade of the south side of James river,
3 shall continue, as heretofore required, to be free for the use of all
4 persons and things going to the canal for the purpose of being trans-
5 ported upon it, or going from the canal immediately after having
6 been transported upon it, and conforming to the lawful rules and re-
7 gulations of the company; but a reasonable toll, within the limit
8 herein before prescribed, may be demanded and collected upon all
9 other persons and things using the same for other purposes.

14. If the said company shall erect a bridge between their canal
2 and the county of Powhatan, at or near the town of Jefferson, or at
3 or near the town of Jackson in the county of Botetourt, no toll shall
4 be charged on said bridges against any person going to or coming
5 from their canal, and the tolls charged upon other persons shall be
6 as the said company may prescribe, not exceeding the rates herein
7 before limited on bridges: and if said bridge at Jefferson be con-
8 structed, then the company are hereby authorized to purchase the
9 ferry at said town.

15. And if said company shall be authorized by law to construct,
2 and shall construct any bridge across any of the rivers on their line
3 of improvement, to accommodate the trade on either side of said
4 rivers, and to enable it to connect with their canal, no tolls shall be

5 charged on any such bridge upon the trade and travel to or from the

6 canal at that point, but they may demand and collect tolls on any

7 other trade and travel which may use the same, not exceeding the

8 tolls which may be assessed on the other bridges herein before

9 limited.

16. In all cases of tolls on any of the company's roads or

2 bridges, return wagons or carts shall pay one-half tolls only; and

3 no toll shall be demanded or received from persons residing within

4 four miles of any gate on any such road, and who shall not have

5 traveled a distance upon said road exceeding four miles. All per-

6 sons on whose land any toll gate may stand, shall be exempt from

7 all tolls at such gate; and persons owning plantations on both sides

8 of any gate, not exceeding four miles distant from each other, shall

9 be exempt from all tolls on their stock, implements of husbandry,

10 and persons employed in conveying the same from one plantation to

11 the other.

17. Persons going to or returning from mill, for the purpose of

2 procuring meal for the consumption of families, shall be exempt

3 from the payment of toll on the Kanawha road and the Blue Ridge

4 turnpike and bridges.

Toll bridges across North river.

18. The said company shall have authority to continue to use

2 their bridges across North river in the county of Rockbridge as toll

3 bridges, and may demand and collect thereat such tolls as they may

4 assess, not exceeding the rates prescribed herein for other bridges.

5 But no tolls shall be collected from the citizens of Rockbridge for
6 crossing the bridge near Lexington.

Tolls on stage coaches.

19. The said company is hereby authorized to regulate from
2 time to time the tolls to be demanded and received on stage coaches
3 running hereafter on the Kanawha turnpike or the Blue Ridge turn-
4 pike.

Bills of lading.

20. Every master of a boat or float conveying property on the
2 water line of the said company shall, on receiving such property on
3 board, cause to be made out a true bill of lading or manifest of such
4 property; which shall be signed by himself and the consignor. The
5 bill is to contain: 1st—The name of the place or milestone at which
6 any of the property therein mentioned was shipped, and the name
7 of the place or milestone to which it is to be cleared: 2d—The num-
8 ber of hogsheads, barrels, boxes, packages, feet of lumber, board
9 measure, bags and bushels of each species of articles: 3d—A speci-
10 fication of the property so shipped by said consignor, and the quan-
11 tity and gross weight of each species. And the legal tolls shall be
12 demandable and payable to the collector of tolls accordingly.

Statement of passengers.

21. The owner or master of every boat used for carrying pas-
2 sengers, shall cause to be made out a statement of the passengers
3 carried in his boat, verified under oath, which he shall deliver to the
4 toll gatherer at the place of his destination; and it shall be lawful

5 for the toll gatherer to whom such statement is returned, to admin-

6 ister the necessary oath for that purpose: which oath, if taken

7 falsely, shall subject the person taking it to the penalties provided

8 by law against persons convicted of forgery.

Collection of tolls.

22. The said company shall, from time to time, cause a list or

2 its rates of toll to be printed, and have such rates posted where

3 they can be readily seen by persons using its work: and when any

4 material change in the rates of toll shall be made, the same shall

5 be advertised in such newspapers as will be most likely to give

6 information thereof to the public; and reasonable notice of such

7 proposed change shall be given before such new tolls shall take

8 effect.

23. A collector of tolls for said company may refuse to let

2 any person or thing pass on the company's works until the toll be

3 paid. If any person or thing pass any toll gate or other proper

4 place for payment, without paying or tendering the toll, such per-

5 son, or the owner or person in possession of such thing, shall forfeit

6 to the company ten dollars. And the like forfeiture shall be in-

7 curred where any person or thing subject to toll is passed through

8 any private gate, bars or fence or other place, for the purpose of

9 evading the payment of the toll. Any such collector knowing of a

10 violation of this section, shall immediately make it known to the

11 president or one of the directors. If he fail so to do, he shall forfeit

11

12 to the company twenty dollars, which may, if so much of his com-
13 pensation remain unpaid, be deducted therefrom.

24. If any collector shall receive for tolls more than is lawful,
2 he shall pay to the party grieved thereby the amount unlawfully
3 received, and two dollars besides. And if said collector shall un-
4 reasonably detain any person or thing at his place of receiving toll,
5 he shall forfeit to the party injured five dollars : Either of which
6 penalties, if the said collector be unable to pay, may be recovered of
7 said company.

25. Every collector shall account for and pay to the proper
2 officer, and at the time prescribed, the tolls which he may have re-
3 ceived from time to time; and for failing to do so, he shall forfeit
4 fifty dollars.

Fines, how recoverable; payment from collectors enforced.

26. Any fine herein imposed shall be recoverable by warrant
2 before a justice of the county or corporation in which the offence
3 was committed; and the said company may also institute and prose-
4 cute any proceedings necessary or proper to enforce payment of
5 what may be due from any collector. Such proceeding may be in
6 the name of the company, in the county or circuit court of the
7 county wherein the collector is employed in the collection of toll,
8 and may be by suit or motion against the collector and his sureties,
9 and his and their personal representatives; and the judgment or
10 decree shall be for the principal sum remaining due, with interest
11 thereon, and fifteen per centum damages.

Tolls on troops.

27. Troops or persons in the military or naval service of this
2 state, with their arms, munitions and baggage, shall have the pre-
3 ference to other persons and property in passing over the line of the
4 company's works, or through or over any of its locks, aqueducts,
5 tunnels or bridges; and the tolls for such troops or persons, and on
6 their arms, munitions and baggage, shall not be more than one-fourth
7 of the rates on other persons or things of like kind. If there be a
8 failure to give any such person or thing passage over the same, in a
9 reasonable time, the said company shall forfeit not less than two nor
10 more than twenty dollars.

Collection of tolls on the Kanawha river.

28. Manifests of the cargoes of all boats or other vessels navi-
2 gating the Kanawha river, shall be filed with the receiver of tolls,
3 designating the names of the cargoes, of their owners, and the mas-
4 ters of the boats or other vessels in which the said cargoes shall be
5 shipped, and of the said boats or vessels, together with that of the
6 shippers and other agents having the control or direction of the said
7 cargoes; and the legal tolls shall be demandable and payable to the
8 collector of tolls accordingly; and in all cases of failure to comply
9 with the regulations hereby established, and to pay the tolls afore-
10 said, it shall be the duty of the said collector to seize and hold the
11 boats or other vessels concerned in the neglect or evasion thereof,
12 until the law is fully complied with; and if that be not done within
13 the space of two days from the time of such seizure, it shall be law-

14 ful for the collector of tolls, after giving five days' previous notice

15 of his intention, by advertisement at the door of the courthouse of

16 the county of Kanawha, to sell at public auction, for ready money,

17 so much of the said cargoes of such boats or vessels as will be suffi-

18 cient to pay the tolls due, with the addition of fifty per cent. thereon,

19 and the necessary expenses incurred by the said collector in seizing,

20 securing and taking care of the said vessels and cargoes; and the

21 said boats or vessels, with the remaining cargoes, and any balances

22 of money which may remain from the sales aforesaid, shall then be

23 returned to the lawful owners or proprietors thereof, or to their

24 agents: and the Virginia canal company, their collectors or agents,

25 may sue out an attachment before any justice of the peace against

26 boats and cargoes upon the Kanawha river for tolls due and unpaid

27 by the said boats and cargoes, their owners, masters or shippers.

     29. The receiver of tolls shall be authorized to board and enter

2 all boats or other vessels in the said river, whether in the stream or

3 at anchor, or at the landings on either shore of the Kanawha river,

4 or the bays or inlets thereof, and to demand and receive the legal

5 tolls on all the commodities contained in the said boats or vessels,

6 whether fully or in part loaded; and in case of failure to pay the

7 said tolls when thus demanded, the said boats or vessels, and the

8 cargoes thereof, shall be liable to seizure, sale and disposition in all

9 respects as prescribed in the foregoing section. And all and every

10 person or persons on board of any boat or other vessel in the said

11 river, refusing or neglecting to come to when required by the said

12 collector to do so, shall forfeit and pay twenty dollars to the use of

13 the said company, to be recovered before any justice of the peace;

14 and all persons resisting the said receiver in the execution of any

15 powers given to him by law, shall be deemed guilty of a misde-

16 meanor, and be prosecuted accordingly.

30. All persons, whether principals or agents, who shall ship off,

2 or authorize to be shipped off, any article subject to the payment of

3 toll, without having first entered the same with the receiver of tolls,

4 as herein prescribed, and paid the tolls due thereon, shall forfeit and

5 pay three times the amount of the tolls on the articles so shipped

6 off, to be recovered for the use of the said company before any jus-

7 tice of the peace.

CHAPTER VII.

OF DIVIDENDS AND LIABILITIES TO STOCKHOLDERS.

Dividends.

1. While the works are in progress, and after they are completed,
2 the Virginia canal company may declare and make semi-annual divi-
3 dends of so much of the surplus profits of their entire work as they
4 may deem it prudent to divide; which shall be paid to the stock-
5 holders, or to their order, in such manner as the by-laws may
6 prescribe.

2. The annual net profits of the company proceeding from all
2 sources, shall never exceed fifteen per centum upon their capital
3 stock; and the tolls shall be regulated from time to time so as to
4 restrain the profits within that limit. All reductions of the tolls
5 made for that purpose, shall be made ratably on every division of
6 the company's line of improvement. The dividends declared as
7 aforesaid upon each share of stock hereafter to be subscribed, shall
8 be in proportion to the amount actually paid thereupon by the stock-
9 holders. But the corporations and individual stockholders at the
10 time of the organization of the company, to whom certificates of
11 stock, upon which the full amount has been paid, shall have been
12 issued, shall be paid dividends, rating the said certificates at one

13 hundred dollars per share.   Those who have not paid in full, shall
14 receive dividends only in proportion to the amount actually paid.

3. Before any dividend shall be declared to others, the annuity
2 to the state of $135,000, and the five per centum per annum agreed
3 to be paid upon the stock owned by the corporations and individuals
4 at the time of the organization of the company, and their assigns,
5 shall be set aside and provided for, as herein prescribed.   And semi-
6 annually, on the first day of January and the first day of July, the
7 said company shall pay into the public treasury of the state, in the
8 mode prescribed by law, the sum of sixty-seven thousand five hun-
9 dred dollars in discharge of said annuity; and at the same periods
10 shall pay to the private stockholders provided for in the sixth article
11 of said agreement, two and a half per cent. on their capital stock,
12 until the line shall have been completed to the Ohio river, when said
13 interest shall cease, and the said private stockholders shall share
14 with the other stockholders the dividends declared by the company.

Proceeding to sequester revenues and property.

4. If the said company shall fail at any time to pay any such
2 semi-annual instalment of said annuity, then out of the sum of one
3 million of dollars deposited in the treasury of the state by the said
4 Virginia canal company, according to the 14th article of the said
5 provisional agreement, as set forth in the 1st chapter, and the interest
6 which may be due thereon, the auditor of the state shall raise and
7 pay into the public treasury the said sum of sixty-seven thousand
8 five hundred dollars, until the said sum of one million of dollars is

9 exhausted. And if after the said sum of one million of dollars is
10 exhausted, the said company shall fail at any time to pay any such
11 annual instalment of said annuity, and it shall remain unpaid for
12 three months after it becomes due, then the auditor of public
13 accounts shall notify the attorney general thereof, who shall imme-
14 diately proceed, on thirty days' notice to the president, treasurer or
15 any director of the said company, to move in the circuit court of
16 the city of Richmond for judgment against such company. Such
17 motion shall have precedence over all other cases; and upon satis-
18 factory proof that the said instalment has not been paid, the said
19 court shall give judgment against said company, and sequester its
20 entire revenues and property; and the Board of public works shall
21 appoint a receiver. The said receiver shall, with the approbation of
22 the Board of public works, appoint all necessary agents to aid him,
23 and shall pay into the treasury such parts of the gross receipts of
24 the company as will pay the amount due, with interest thereon;
25 whereupon the sequestration shall wholly cease and determine; but
26 during such sequestration the said receiver and his agents shall,
27 under the direction of the Board of public works, be paid for their
28 services out of such receipts.

5. If the said company shall fail to pay to any of the said pri-
2 vate stockholders the semi-annual interest on their stock for five
3 days after the same is demanded, upon the application of such stock-
4 holders, upon ten days' notice, to any officer or director of the com-
5 pany, at the office of the company in Richmond, the auditor of the

6 state shall raise and pay the said interest due, out of the said sum

7 of one million of dollars deposited in the treasury by the said com-

8 pany, and charge the same to the company: or the said stockholders

9 or any of them may, at their option, proceed, by warrant before a

10 justice of the peace, to recover the same, if the justice have jurisdic-

11 tion of the amount, or if not, by action of debt in the said circuit

12 court. And when the said work shall be completed to the Ohio river

13 as aforesaid, the payment of the said five per cent. per annum shall

14 cease.

6. The dividends which may be payable to the commonwealth

2 of Virginia upon the stock held by the state, in trust for individuals

3 who failed or refused to receive the same, shall be paid, as other

4 public dues to the state are paid, to the treasurer of the state, upon

5 demand.

Dividends, where to be paid.

7. The dividends and other dues to the American stockholders,

2 other than those herein before provided for, shall be paid at the com-

3 pany's office in the city of Richmond. Those of the foreign stock-

4 holders may be paid in Paris, or elsewhere, as may be prescribed by

5 the by-laws of the company.

Dividends to be credited against debts.

8. If any stockholder be indebted to the company, his dividend,

2 or so much as may be necessary, shall be passed to his credit in

3 payment of the debt.

When directors liable for illegal dividend.

9. If the board shall declare a dividend of any part of the capi-

12

2 tal stock of the company, all the members of the board who shall be
3 present, and not dissent therefrom, shall, in their individual capacity,
4 be jointly and severally liable to the company's creditors for the
5 amount of capital so divided, and may be decreed against therefor,
6 on a bill in equity, filed on behalf of such creditors; and, moreover,
7 each stockholder who shall participate in such dividend, shall be
8 liable to such creditors to the extent of the capital stock so received
9 by him.

Notice of dividend to be published; uncalled for dividends to be paid into state treasury.

10. Of every dividend declared, and of the time and place ap-
2 pointed for the payment thereof, the board shall cause notice to be
3 published in some newspaper printed in the city of Richmond, and
4 shall also give notice thereof in such manner as they may deem ex-
5 pedient, in the city of Paris. In January, 1865, and once in every
6 five years thereafter, they shall publish in like manner a list of all
7 dividends which have remained unpaid for two years or more, with
8 the names of the persons to whose credit such dividends stand. All
9 dividends not called for within the term of five years after they have
10 been declared, shall be paid into the public treasury, to be subject
11 to the order of the shareholder or his legal representative, when
12 called for, the shareholder establishing his right thereto, to the satis-
13 faction of the auditor of public accounts.

CHAPTER VIII.

REGULATION FOR THE INSPECTION OF BOATS, AND FOR BOATMEN AND OTHERS; HARBOR AND DOCK MASTERS; TO PREVENT THE COMPANY'S WORKMEN OR EMPLOYEES FROM VIOLATING THE PEACE; EXEMPTING THEM FROM WORKING ON OTHER ROADS, AND FROM MILITIA DUTY.

Inspectors of boats.

1. The said company may require such of the lock keepers or
2 toll gatherers upon any part of their water line as they may invest
3 with the authority hereby given, to become inspectors of boats, and
4 require from such person bond with good security in such penalty as
5 their by-laws may prescribe, for the true and faithful performance
6 of the duties of his office; and such person shall also take an oath
7 for the same purpose.

Dock masters and harbor masters.

2. The said Virginia canal company may establish regulations
2 for the preservation of good order at any of their basins, docks or
3 landings, and at wharfs for loading and unloading boats or vessels
4 engaged in navigating their water line, at any point thereon, whether
5 on rivers or canal: provided such regulations be consistent with the
6 laws of the state and the police regulations of any city or corpora-
7 tion authorized by law to prescribe such regulations; and for such

8 purpose may appoint dock masters or other officers, whose duty it
9 shall be to cause such regulations to be obeyed, and to collect the
10 penalties fixed by such regulations for the infringements thereof:
11 which penalties shall be recoverable before any tribunal having
12 jurisdiction thereof.

3. No harbor master shall have any control over any boat or
2 vessel after the same shall have entered the said company's line as
3 designated in the fifth chapter, nor while entering, remaining in or
4 leaving any of said company's docks, locks or water line, or any
5 channel leading thereto, which have been constructed by them ac-
6 cording to law, or by the company whose rights and interests have
7 been transferred to them.

4. The said dock masters, or other officers appointed to dis-
2 charge their duties, shall regulate the anchoring and mooring of all
3 lighters, boats, and bay and river craft, steam boats and other ves-
4 sels which come within any of said docks or basins, or anchor at or
5 are secured at any of such wharfs or landings. He shall also regu-
6 late their entrances and departure, so as to prevent confusion and
7 disorder.

5. Any master or head man of any vessel, or boat or other craft,
2 who shall fail or refuse to obey, or comply with the lawful order of
3 any of said dock masters or other officers, after having had a rea-
4 sonable time for obedience or compliance, shall be liable to a fine of
5 five dollars for every such offence, to be recovered before any justice
6 of the peace having jurisdiction.

To prevent company's employees from violating the peace.

6. If at any time, on any part of the company's line, any work-
2 man or other employee shall be engaged in a riotous, tumultuous or
3 unlawful assembly, or in any violation of the peace, any judge or
4 justice within his jurisdiction may suppress the same ; and for that
5 purpose may command the assistance of all. persons present, and of
6 the sheriff or sergeant of the county or corporation, with his posse,
7 if need be, to arrest and secure those engaged in any violation of
8 the peace.   And it shall be the duty of any contractor or officer of
9 the said company having knowledge thereof, to give immediate in-
10 formation of any such violation or apprehended violation, to some
11 judge or justice nearest thereto.   Any person so arrested shall be
12 proceeded against as prescribed by law in such cases.

Exemption from working on other roads.

7. The officers, contractors and their agents and laborers, hire-
2 lings or hands, while engaged at work upon the line of the com-
3 pany's works, shall be exempt from, and in no wise subject to the
4 provisions of any road law, by which the citizens of any county or
5 corporation along said line may be compelled to perform labor on
6 any road or work within the same, and from any tax or contribution
7 whatever, under any special road law heretofore passed, or that may
8 be hereafter passed for any county or corporation.

Exemption from militia duty.

8. The following persons shall be exempt from the performance
2 of the ordinary duties of militiamen, but shall be liable to be drafted

94   Bill No. 197.

3 and detailed for actual service, to wit: All ferrymen employed by
4 said company at any ferry owned by it; all keepers of any toll
5 bridge owned in like manner; two of the clerks in the office of col-
6 lector of tolls on the Richmond dock and on the lower section of
7 the company's canal; the inspectors of boats, lock gate keepers and
8 overseers employed by them; all their toll gatherers, and the work-
9 men who are non-residents of the county or corporation in which
10 they are at work, and actually engaged in fulfilling any contract for
11 the completion of any work on the company's water line in a speci-
12 fied time.

CHAPTER IX.

FOR THE PREVENTION OF OBSTRUCTIONS; TO FACILITATE NAVIGATION
ON THE COMPANY'S LINE, AND TO PUNISH OFFENDERS; SALE OF
WATER POWER; RESERVATION OF WATER FOR THE STATE ARMORIES.

Rights of navigation preserved; limitation on power of courts to grant
leave to erect dams.

1. In any of the rivers or water courses, the right of improving
2 or extending the navigation of which has been given hereby, or may
3 be hereafter given to the Virginia canal company, it shall not be
4 lawful for any court to grant to any other person or company the
5 preference to the use of the water flowing therein for the purposes
6 of such navigation, nor to grant leave to any person to erect a dam
7 or other obstruction across or in such water course, by which the
8 ordinary navigation will be obstructed, nor by which the water used
9 as a feeder to any part of the company's water line may be diverted
10 or lessened, without the consent of said company. Any such dam
11 or obstruction, notwithstanding it may be built under such leave,
12 shall be deemed a nuisance, and may be abated as such.

Penalty for obstructing navigation with fish traps, &c.

2. If any person or company shall hereafter make or cause to be
2 made any hedges, fish traps or other obstructions in any of said
3 rivers composing part of the said company's water line, so as to

4 impede or injure the passage of batteaux, floats or other vessels,
5 such person or company shall forfeit and pay the sum of fifty dollars
6 for each offence.

Penalty for trespasses on works or property of company.

3. If any person shall willfully trespass on the possessions or
2 do injury to the works or other property of the company, he shall
3 be deemed guilty of a misdemeanor, and be punished accordingly,
4 except in those cases in which the offence is of a higher grade, or
5 otherwise specifically punished by law.

Penalty for injuring or obstructing roads, bridges, &c.

4. Any person who shall knowingly and willfully, without law-
2 ful authority, break down, destroy or injure any bridge, bench or
3 log placed across a stream for the accommodation, or any sign-
4 board, milestone or post for the direction of travelers, or obstruct
5 any road or bridge, or any ditch made for the purpose of draining
6 any road belonging to said company, or destroy or injure any of
7 said company's boundary stones or monuments to define the limits
8 of their property, such person shall be punished by fine, at the dis-
9 cretion of a jury.

Burning a bridge, dam, &c. or a vessel.

5. If a free person maliciously burn any bridge, lock, dam, or
2 any ship, boat or other vessel, or any of the company's construc-
3 tions, of the value of one hundred dollars or more, he shall be con-
4 fined in the penitentiary not less than three nor more than ten years ;
5 and if the value be less than one hundred dollars, he shall be con-

6 fined in jail not exceeding one year, and be fined not exceeding two
7 hundred dollars.

Injurying canal, &c.

6. If a free person maliciously obstruct, remove, destroy or in-
2 jure any part of the company's canal or roads, or any of its con-
3 structions, or any bridge or fixture thereof, or any part of its water
4 line, or obstruct, remove destroy or injure any machinery, work or
5 engine thereof, he shall be punished by fine, at the discretion of a
6 jury. And if the life of any traveler on the company's water line
7 or roads and bridges be put in peril by any such offence, the offen
8 der shall be confined in the penitentiary not less than three nor more
9 than five years.

Injury in public conveyance.

7. If any driver, conductor or captain of any vehicle, or boat
2 or other vessel for public conveyance, being free, shall, in the man-
3 agement of such vehicle, or boat or other vessel, willfully or negli-
4 gently inflict bodily injury on any person, he shall be punished as
5 for a misdemeanor.

Buoys, beacons and ring bolts to be placed in rivers.

8. The said company shall cause buoys to be placed in any part
2 of their water line in which they may be necessary, so as readily
3 and clearly to indicate and point out to navigators all the en-
4 trances and lines of the sluices, the wing dams and the jetties,
5 and generally the course of the channels. They shall also cause
6 beacons to be placed on the bars, rocks and other obstructions to
                         13

7 navigation, not within the sluices or channels, but which, from their
8 positions, or from other causes, are likely to endanger the safety of
9 vessels or boats navigating the said water line; which buoys and
10 beacons shall be so constructed as to be visible, until the water in
11 any of the rivers on the said line in which they may be necessary,
12 shall rise five feet above its ordinary lowest level. For the greater
13 safety and convenience of the trade, it shall be the further duty of
14 the said company to cause large rings to be attached by suitable
15 bolts to rocks or other stable bodies, along the sluices and at the
16 ends of the wing dams and jetties, for the better enabling boats or
17 vessels to overcome the force of the currents by warps and cords.

Water not to be used but for navigation; water power, how sold.

9. The water, or any part thereof, conveyed through any canal
2 or cut made by the company, except where the land between the
3 canal and river is entirely the property of the company, shall not
4 be used for any purpose but navigation, unless the consent of the
5 proprietors of the land be first had; but the company may lease or
6 sell to any person or company the water power necessary for pro-
7 pelling any machinery for milling or other purposes, where such
8 person or company may have obtained the necessary site therefor.
9 And where the company is possessed of, or may acquire hereafter,
10 land as herein before provided for, and shall not thereby damage
11 other proprietors of land in a manner not compensated for at the
12 time of acquiring the same, they may establish any such machinery,
13 and work the same with the water from any canal or dam, so as not

14 to impair the navigation by such use of water, and may again sell or
15 lease the same.

Water for armory, &c. reserved.

20. The commonwealth of Virginia reserves the right to the use
2 of so much of the water in the canal of the company as may be
3 sufficient to propel the machinery necessary for the manufacturing
4 of arms at the public armory in the city of Richmond, free of all
5 charge whatever; and the company shall at no time stop or obstruct
6 the use of said water, except when absolutely necessary for the re-
7 pair of the canal; and in time of war or apprehended danger, the
8 governor shall be the judge of such necessity. The said company
9 shall not obstruct the use of the water to the extent it is now en-
10 joyed to the lessees of the state on the property adjoining the said
11 armory, they paying the rent for said water heretofore agreed to be
12 paid, or that may be contracted to be paid in case of a renewal of
13 their lease: provided, that the quantity of water taken by the state
14 shall not so reduce the water in the canal as to interfere with the
15 navigation thereof, and the compliance by the company with any
16 contract heretofore made for a supply of water from the canal to the
17 mills or other manufactories.

CHAPTER X.

Reports required of company.

1. The Virginia canal company shall make an annual report to
2 the Board of public works of its condition and the state of its affairs
3 on the 30th day of September, and of the operations of the com-
4 pany during the year ending on that day; which report shall be
5 verified by the president of the company, and be filed in the office
6 of the said board by the 15th day of November in each year. The
7 said report shall be in such form as the Board of public works shall
8 prescribe; and in preparing such form, the said board are hereby
9 directed to require that the said report shall contain as full and mi-
10 nute information in regard to the condition, affairs and operations
11 of the said canal company, as may be required by said board in
12 regard to the condition, affairs and operations of the railroad com-
13 panies within this commonwealth.

Penalty for failing to make report.

2. If the said canal company shall fail to make the report herein
2 required, and in the manner required, it shall be liable to a penalty

3 not exceeding five hundred dollars. And the Board of public works,
4 if in session, or its secretary, if it be not in session, shall report such
5 failure immediately to the attorney general; and it shall be his duty,
6 after giving to the said company ten days' notice, to proceed against
7 the same for such failure, by motion in the circuit court of the city
8 of Richmond. Such court shall consider said case a privileged case,
9 and it shall be its duty to enter up a judgment for a fine not exceed-
10 ing five hundred dollars and the costs, including a fee of twenty
11 dollars for the services of said attorney general. Execution shall
12 be awarded against the said company, to be levied as other execu-
13 tions are levied upon any of its property.

Report of number of passengers.

3. The said canal company shall hereafter report quarterly, on
2 the 15th day of March, June, September and December in each year,
3 to the auditor of public accounts, the number of passengers trans-
4 ported, and the aggregate number of miles traveled by them within
5 the commonwealth, and the gross amount of tolls received for the
6 transportation of freight over its water line, or any part thereof,
7 and over its roads and bridges, during the quarter of the year next
8 preceding the first day of the month in which such report is made.

Penalty for failure, how recoverable.

4. Such statement shall be verified by the oath of the secretary.
2 If the said company shall fail to make such report, it shall be liable
3 to a fine not exceeding five hundred dollars, to be recovered by the
4 attorney general as herein before prescribed. At the time of making

5 such report, the company shall pay into the treasury, for every pas-
6 senger liable to toll, who may be transported along its water line or
7 over its roads or bridges, a tax at the rate of one mill for every mile
8 of transportation of each of such passengers, and a tax of one-half
9 of one per centum of such gross amount of tolls received for the
10 transportation of freights. The said company, upon the payment
11 of such taxes, shall not be assessed with any tax on its franchises,
12 tolls, lands, buildings, bridges, boats or other property, which they
13 are authorized by law to hold or have. But if it shall fail to pay
14 the said taxes at the times specified therefor, then its lands, buildings,
15 bridges, boats and other property shall be immediately assessed
16 under the directions of the auditor of public accounts, by any per-
17 son appointed by him for the purpose, at the full value; and a tax
18 shall at once be levied thereon as on real estate and on other pro-
19 perty, to be collected by any sheriff whom the auditor may direct;
20 and such sheriff shall distrain and sell any personal property of
21 such company, and pay such taxes into the treasury within three
22 months from the time when such assessment is furnished to him.

Duration of charter.

5. If the said Virginia canal company be not organized by the
2 appointment of a president and directors as required by this charter,
3 within nine months from the passage, and bona fide commence its
4 works within six months after its organization, or if, after commenc-
5 ing its works, it shall suspend its operations for one year, or if it
6 shall fail to comply with the provisions of the fifth chapter hereof,

7 so far as the same refers to the fourteenth article of the said pro-

8 visional agreement, the general assembly may abrogate this charter,

9 and declare that the corporate rights and privileges of the company

10 shall cease; or it may allow said company such further time to com-

11 plete the said works and to comply with its engagements, as to the

12 legislature may seem just and proper.

Disposition of property when corporation is dissolved.

6. If the said corporation shall be dissolved as aforesaid, and its

2 corporate rights and privileges shall have ceased, all its works and

3 property, and debts due to it, shall be subject to the payment of

4 debts due by it, in accordance with the provisions of this charter;

5 and it may sue and be sued as before for the purpose of collecting

6 debts due to it, prosecuting rights under previous contracts with it,

7 and enforcing its liabilities and transferring its property and debts

8 to its successor, as hereafter provided.

When James river and Kanawha company restored to its rights.

7. If the said Virginia canal company shall fail to comply with

2 its undertaking as herein before set out, so that the general assembly

3 shall proceed to abrogate its charter and to declare that its corporate

4 rights and privileges shall cease, and that its property shall be for-

5 feited according to the provisions of this act and said provisional

6 agreement, then the James river and Kanawha company, as it

7 existed before the passage of this act, shall thereupon be restored

8 to all the rights conferred by its charter and the laws existing at the

9 time of the passage of this act, as fully and effectually as if this act

10 had never passed; and it shall then be lawful for the said James

11 river and Kanawha company to issue bonds under the act of the

12 23d day of March, 1860, to the said E. de Bellot des Minieres, for

13 himself and associates, under the firm and style of Bellot des Min-

14 ieres, Brothers and Company, of France, and their assigns, for an

15 amount equal to the principal sum which may have been advanced

16 by them and expended upon the works mentioned in this act, and the

17 interest thereon from the time when the same shall have been

18 expended until the repayment in bonds as aforesaid: provided the

19 amount authorized to be issued by the said act be sufficient therefor.

8. The stockholders in the Virginia canal company, at the time

2 when its said charter shall cease, and when the rights of the said

3 company shall be transferred to the said James river and Kanawha

4 company, who were stockholders in the James river and Kanawha

5 company, or who derived title to their stock from or under such

6 stockholders, to the extent of the stock so held, shall be considered

7 stockholders in that company, and their stock shall be of the par

8 value at which it was estimated while stockholders of the said James

9 river and Kanawha company; and in all other respects they shall

10 be restored to their rights and liabilities, and be entitled to the

11 profits and remedies granted by the charter of the said James river

12 and Kanawha company before the passage of this act. And the

13 state shall have the same quantity of stock in the said James river

14 and Kanawha company, and the same interest therein as is now held

15 by the state in said company.

BILL No. 199.

P.
154
CV. 2287-6

SENATE BILL.

A BILL

Amending the third section of chapter seven of the Code of Virginia.

1. Be it enacted by the General Assembly of Virginia, That the
2 third section of chapter seven of the Code of Virginia, be amended
3 and re-enacted so as to read as follows:

4   "§3. There shall be elected by the voters in each county a clerk
5 of the county court, a surveyor, an attorney for the Commonwealth, a
6 sheriff and a commissioner or so many commissioners of the revenue
7 as may be authorized by law; and in each of the corporations of
8 Richmond, Fredericksburg, Lynchburg, Winchester, Danville, Staun-
9 ton and Williamsburg, by the voters thereof respectively, a commis-
10 sioner of the revenue, or so many commissioners as may be author-
11 ized by law.   In each city for which a circuit court is held, a clerk
12 for such court; in the city of Richmond, a sheriff; in each county in
13 which a circuit court is held, an attorney for the Commonwealth
14 and a clerk for such courts.   In each district laid off by commis-
15 sioners under the act providing for the districting the counties,
16 passed April second, eighteen hundred and fifty-two, four justices of
17 the peace; in every such district one constable, except in the fourth

18 district in the county of Greenbrier, in which by the order of the

19 county court of said county, two constables may be elected; and ex-

20 cept also in the tenth district of the county of Albemarle, in which

21 by the order of the county court of said last named county, an ad-

22 ditional constable may at any time be elected. And in every such

23 district by the voters without the limits of a town that provides for

24 its poor, one overseer, or such additional number as the court of the

25 county may direct. Said election shall be held for such clerks and

26 surveyors in the sixth year; for such justices of the peace, attorneys

27 for the Commonwealth and overseers of the poor, on the same day in

28 every fourth year; and for sheriffs and commissioners of the revenue

29 on the same day in every second year; counting in each case from

30 the fourth Thursday in May, eighteen hundred and fifty-two: pro-

31 vided, that the constables elected under this act shall have power to

32 perform the duties of their office in districts other than those in which

33 they are elected; and provided further, that the voters of the cities of

34 Norfolk, Petersburg and Williamsburg, and of the towns of Frede-

35 ricksburg, Lynchburg, Winchester and Danville, shall not be author-

36 ized to vote for a surveyor for the several counties in which they are

37 respectively located."

2. This act shall be in force from its passage.

SENATE BILL.

———

A BILL

Imposing taxes for the support of government.

1. Be it enacted by the general assembly, That the taxes on the
2 persons and subjects in this chapter mentioned, or required by law
3 to be listed or assessed, shall be yearly as follows :

Taxes on lands and lots.

4   On tracts of lands and lots, with the improvements thereon, not
5 exempt from taxation, forty cents on every hundred dollars value
6 thereof; and herein shall be included all tracts of lands and lots,
7 with the improvements thereon, not otherwise taxed, or exempt from
8 taxation, of incorporated joint stock companies, savings institutions
9 and insurance companies.

On personal property.

2. On all the personal property, moneys and credits, as defined
2 in this section, including all capital, personal property and moneys
3 of incorporated joint stock companies (other than railroad, canal or
4 turnpike companies), and all capital invested, used or employed in
5 any manufacturing, trade or other business, forty cents on every
6 hundred dollars value thereof.   But slaves, and property otherwise

7 taxed, and property from which any income so taxed is derived, or
8 on the capital invested in any trade or business in respect to which
9 a license so taxed is issued, certificates of stock, moneys and per-
10 sonal property that constitute part of the capital of any bank,
11 savings institutions and insurance companies, whether incorporated
12 by this or any other state, which have declared dividends, within
13 one year preceding the first day of February, of as much as six per
14 cent. profits, shall not be taxed under the provisions of this section.
15 The word "moneys" shall be construed to include not only gold,
16 silver and copper coins, but bullion and bank notes. The word
17 "credits" shall be construed to mean all bank, state or corporation
18 stocks, claims or demands owing or coming to any person, whether
19 due or not, and whether payable in money or other thing. Moneys
20 and credits owned by any resident of this state, whether such
21 moneys or credits are within or without this state, shall be taxed at
22 the rate prescribed by this section.

On slaves.

3. On every slave who has attained the age of twelve years,
2 whether owned or hired, or whether exempted from county levy in
3 consequence of bodily infirmity or not, one dollar and twenty cents;
4 and no company exempted by this chapter from taxation, shall be
5 entitled to any such exemption from taxation of any slave acquired
6 since the adoption of the constitution, or by any law, exempting the
7 property of railroad or canal companies, upon the payment of taxes
8 on freight or passengers.

On free negroes.

4. On every male free negro who has attained the age of twenty-
2 one years, eighty cents; but no tax shall hereafter be assessed or
3 collected on such male free negro, under the act of the 6th of April
4 1853, establishing a colonization board.

On white males.

5. On every white male inhabitant who has attained the age of
2 twenty-one years, not exempted from taxation by order of court in
3 consequence of bodily infirmity, eighty cents.

On public bonds.

6. On the interest or profit which may have accrued, and is
2 solvent, or which may have been received by any person, or con-
3 verted into principal so as to become an interest-bearing subject, or
4 otherwise appropriated, within the year next preceding the first day
5 of February of each year, arising from bonds and certificates of
6 debt of this or any other state, or country, or any corporation cre-
7 ated by this or any other state, whether the stock of such company
8 be exempt from taxation or not, six and two-thirds per centum. But
9 such interests or profits derived from bank stock or shares of savings
10 institutions and insurance companies which pay taxes thereon into
11 the treasury, shall not be included herein, unless invested or other-
12 wise appropriated; and if so invested or otherwise appropriated, the
13 tax thereon shall be at the rate of forty cents upon every hundred
14 dollars value thereof. If no interest shall have been received within
15 the year preceding the first day of February, then the value of the

16 principal of such bonds shall be assessed and taxed as other pro-
17 perty.

On bank dividends.

7. On the dividends declared by any bank incorporated by this
2 state, the tax shall be six and two-thirds per centum upon the amount
3 thereof, to be paid into the treasury by the bank. If the dividend
4 be that of a bank incorporated elsewhere, the tax shall be six and
5 two-thirds per centum upon the amount thereof, to be assessed and
6 collected as other taxes.

On dividends of savings institutions and insurance companies.

8. On the dividends declared within the year preceding the first
2 day of February, if the same be equal to or over six per centum on
3 its capital, by savings institutions and insurance companies, to be
4 paid by such institutions and companies into the treasury respec-
5 tively, six and two-thirds per centum; but if such dividend be not
6 equal to six per centum of such capital, then its capital shall be
7 listed and taxed as other property.

On income.

9. On the income, salary or fees received during the year ending
2 the first day of February of each year, arising from any calling,
3 service or profession, or in consideration of the discharge of any
4 office or employment in the service of the state, or in consideration
5 of the discharge of any office or employment in the service of any
6 corporation, or in the service of any company, firm or person, except
7 where the service is that of a minister of the gospel, one-half of
8 one per centum on so much thereof as exceeds two hundred and fifty

9 dollars and not more than five hundred dollars; one per centum if
10 the same be five hundred dollars. The tax on a salary payable
11 under this section by an officer of government receiving the same
12 out of the treasury, shall be deducted from the amount drawn by
13 the treasury at the time the salary is audited and paid; and fees or
14 other income of such officer shall be listed and assessed by the com-
15 missioner as in other cases, at the rates prescribed thereon.

On toll bridges.

10. On the yearly rent or annual value of toll bridges and fer-
2 ries other than those toll bridges and ferries exempt by their charter
3 from taxation, six per centum.

On collateral inheritances.

11. On the estate of a decedent, which passes under his will, or
2 by descent to any other person, or for any other use than to or for
3 the use of the father, mother, husband, wife, brother, sister or lineal
4 descendant of such decedent, there shall be a tax of two per centum
5 of such estate; and no estate shall hereafter so descend or so pass
6 until the said tax shall be paid. Any taxes which would have ac-
7 crued under this section, had it existed and been in force since the
8 passage of the act imposing taxes for the support of government,
9 on the 18th day of March 1856, shall, where the estate has been
10 paid over, be assessed with interest, as omitted taxes against the
11 owner. All such assessments are to be made by the commissioner
12 as on other subjects. There shall be included as omitted taxes on
13 said estates, all such taxes as were heretofore released, by order of
14 court, as erroneously assessed.

Internal improvement companies.

12. Every rail road company or canal company shall hereafter
2 report quarterly, on the fifteenth day of March, June, September
3 and December in each year, to the auditor of public accounts, the
4 number of passengers transported, and the aggregate number of
5 miles traveled by them within this commonwealth, and the gross
6 amount received by such company for the transportation of freight
7 over such road or canal, or any part thereof, or over water or other
8 improvement, owned or connected therewith, during the quarter of
9 the year next preceding the first day of the month in which such re-
10 port is to be made. Such company, whose road or canal is only in
11 part within the commonwealth, shall report as aforesaid such portion
12 only of such amount received for the transportation of freight, as
13 the part of the said road or canal, which is within this common-
14 wealth, bears to the whole of such road or canal. If the profits of
15 such road or canal consist, in whole or in part of tolls, the gross
16 amount thereof shall, for the purposes of this act, be construed to
17 be a part of the gross amount received for the transportation of
18 freight.

13. Such statement shall be verified by the oaths of the presi-
2 dent and the superintendent of transportation, or other proper offi-
3 cer. Every company failing to make such report, shall be fined five
4 hundred dollars; and any company having a subordinate board, or
5 any other board managing any part of its works, may by its by-laws
6 create and enforce such penalties as will secure proper reports to

7 such companies. At the time of making such report, the company

8 shall pay into the treasury, for every passenger transported, a tax

9 at the rate of one mill for every mile of transportation of each of

10 such passengers, and a tax of one-half of one per centum of such

11 gross amount received for the transportation of freights and tolls.

12 Every such company paying such taxes, shall not be assessed with

13 any tax on its lands, buildings, cars, boats or other property (other

14 than slaves) which they are authorized by law to hold or have. But

15 if any such company fail to pay such taxes at either of the terms

16 specified therefor, then its lands, buildings, cars, boats and other

17 property shall be immediately assessed under the directions of the

18 auditor of public accounts, by any person appointed by him for the

19 purpose, at its full value, and a tax shall at once be levied thereon

20 as on real estate and other property, at ten cents on every hundred

21 dollars value, on account of each quarterly default, to be collected

22 by any sheriff whom the auditor may direct, and such sheriff shall

23 distrain and sell any personal property of such company, and pay

24 such taxes into the treasury within three months from the time when

25 such assessment is furnished to him.

Express companies.

14. Every express company, in addition to the license tax on

2 such company on any express business, shall make a return to the

3 auditor of public accounts, on the 15th day of June and December

4 in each year, of the total receipts of such company, on account of

5 its operations within the state of Virginia within the six months

6 preceding the first day of June and December in each year. Such
7 returns shall be verified by the oaths of the agent and chief officers
8 of such company, at its principal office or offices in this state,
9 in the manner and according to the forms prescribed by the said
10 auditor, whether collected within or without the state. Such express
11 company shall pay on the total receipts so reported, a tax of one-
12 half of one per centum, except for the transportation of bank notes
13 for brokers and non-residents, for which the tax shall be one-fourth
14 of one per cent. upon the amount of bank notes transported; and
15 for failure to make such report or pay such tax, a penalty of six
16 hundred dollars shall be imposed on the company so failing, to be
17 recovered as other penalties are: provided, however, that no express
18 company, through any of its agents, shall transact any business ap-
19 pertaining to the business of a broker, unless it be for the common-
20 wealth. Each principal officer shall require from the several agents
21 employed by such company, a report of their transactions on oath,
22 which report so sworn to shall accompany the report of the chief
23 officer to the auditor.

On suits.

15. When any orignal suit, attachment (other than an attach-
2 ment sued out under the provisions of the 11th section of chapter
3 188 of the Code), or other action is commenced in a circuit, county
4 or corporation court, there shall be a tax of one dollar; if it be an
5 appeal, writ of error or supersedeas in a circuit court, there shall be
6 a tax of two dollars; if it be an appeal, writ of error or supersedeas

7 in a district court, three dollars and fifty cents; and if in a court of

8 appeals, five dollars: And all actions brought in any court, whether

9 process be issued from court in the first place or not, shall be sub-

10 ject to said tax.

On seals.

16. When the seal of a court, of a notary public, or the seal of

2 the state is annexed to any paper, except in those cases exempted

3 by law, the taxes shall be as follows: For the seal of the state, two

4 dollars: for any other seal, one dollar and fifty cents, except in

5 cases of protests of bills or notes for one hundred dollars or smaller

6 sums: in which cases, the tax shall be fifty cents; and herein shall

7 be included a tax on a scroll annexed to a paper in lieu of an official

8 seal.

On wills and administrations.

17. On the probate of every will or grant of administration,

2 there shall be a tax of dollar.

Deeds.

18. On every deed admitted to record, whether the same has

2 been recorded before or not, and on every contract relating to real

3 estate, whether it be a deed or not, which is admitted to record,

4 there shall be a tax of one dollar.

ON LICENSES.

Ordinaries.

19. The taxes on licences shall be as follows:

2 On a license to keep an ordinary or house of public entertain-

3 ment, forty dollars; and if the yearly value of such house and

4 furniture, whether rented or kept by the proprietor, exceeds one

5 hundred dollars, and is less than two hundred dollars, the tax shall

6 be fifty dollars; and if the yearly value thereof exceeds two hun-

7 dred dollars, there shall be added to the last mentioned sum fifteen

8 per cent. on so much thereof as exceeds two hundred dollars: And

9 if the license grants the privilege of retailing ardent spirits, porter,

10 ale or beer, to be drank elsewhere than at such ordinary, there shall

11 be added to said license a tax of fifty dollars in addition to the

12 amount otherwise imposed; and if the business be continued, there

13 shall also be a tax of one per centum upon the amount of such sales

14 for the preceding year, in addition to the specific tax.

Private entertainment.

20. On a license to keep a house of private entertainment or a

2 private boarding house, or any other house not private, but kept for

3 public resort for any purpose, five dollars; and if the yearly value

4 of such house and furniture exceed fifty dollars and is less than one

5 hundred dollars, the tax shall be ten dollars. If the yearly value

6 thereof exceed one hundred dollars, there shall be added to the last

7 mentioned sum ten per cent. on so much thereof as exceeds one

8 hundred dollars. But no house shall be deemed a private boarding

9 house with less than five boarders.

21. On every license to keep a cook shop or eating house, fifteen

2 dollars; and in addition thereto, fifteen per cent. on so much of the

3 yearly value thereof as exceeds one hundred dollars.

Bowling alleys.

22. On every license permitting a bowling alley or saloon to be
2 kept for a year, fifty dollars: and if there is more than one such
3 alley kept in any one room, fifteen dollars each shall be charged for
4 the excess over one.

Billiard tables.

23. On every license permitting a billiard table to be kept for a
2 year, one hundred dollars: provided, that where there is more than
3 one such table kept in any one room, fifty dollars each shall be
4 charged for the excess over one table : provided, that if such billiard
5 table, bowling alley or saloon, be not kept open more than four
6 months in any one year, the taxes thereon shall only be one-half of
7 these rates, but the license granted shall, at the time of granting
8 the same, be for a period of four months, or for a period of twelve
9 months.

Bagatelle tables.

24. On every license permitting a bagatelle or other like table
2 to be kept for one year or any less time, twenty dollars for the first,
3 and if more than one, ten dollars for the second, and five dollars for
4 each additional table kept in the same house.

Livery stables.

25. On every license to a keeper of a livery stable, one dollar
2 for each stall thereof; and herein shall be included as stalls, such
3 space as may be necessary for a horse to stand, and in which a
4 horse is or may be kept, and no exemption from this license shall

5 be allowed to any person in consequence of such person being
6 licensed to keep an ordinary or house of private entertainment, if
7 any horses be kept there or be fed or hired for compensation by the
8 proprietor thereof; but no tax shall be required for such horses as
9 belong to travelers stopping at such house.

Distilleries.

26. On every license to the proprietor of a distillery, if a
2 beginner, the tax shall be twenty dollars; and if said distillery is to
3 be kept in operation as much as four months in the year, the tax
4 shall be thirty dollars; if for six months, forty dollars; if for nine
5 months, sixty dollars; if for a longer time than nine months, one
6 hundred dollars; and if such distillery has been kept in operation
7 as much as four months in the year next preceding the time of
8 obtaining such license, the proprietor thereof shall pay, in addition
9 to the tax imposed on beginners, one per centum on the amount of
10 sales of liquors so manufactured at such distillery for the twelve
11 months next preceding the time of obtaining such license. No com-
12 pany or firm, whether engaged in distilling grain or fruit produced
13 by themselves or not, owning a distillery, shall be exempt from
14 taxation, unless the grain or fruit was the joint production of the
15 company or firm owning the distillery. If the distillery is engaged
16 in distilling fruit or grain produced by the owner thereof, and is not
17 so engaged for more than four months, no tax shall be imposed; but
18 if so engaged for more than four months, whether engaged in dis-
19 tilling fruit or grain produced by the owner or not, the tax shall be
20 assessed and collected as in this section provided.

Merchants.

27. On every license to a merchant or mercantile firm, where a
2 specific tax is to be paid, sixty dollars: provided, that if the capital
3 employed and to be employed, including borrowed capital and goods
4 and property bought on credit, by said merchant or firm be shown
5 by affidavit to be less than five hundred dollars, the tax to be paid
6 shall be ten dollars; but this proviso shall not authorize any such
7 person to sell wine, ardent spirits, or a mixture thereof; and when
8 the tax is in proportion to the sales, if the taxable sales shall be
9 under one thousand and one dollars, the tax shall be twenty dollars;
10 if one thousand and one and under fifteen hundred dollars, twenty-
11 four dollars; if fifteen hundred dollars and under twenty-five hun-
12 dred dollars, thirty-two dollars; if twenty-five hundred dollars and
13 under five thousand dollars, forty-eight dollars; if five thousand
14 dollars and under ten thousand dollars, seventy-six dollars; if ten
15 thousand and under fifteen thousand dollars, ninety-six dollars; if
16 fifteen thousand dollars and under twenty thousand dollars, one
17 hundred and twelve dollars; if twenty thousand dollars and under
18 thirty thousand dollars, one hundred and forty dollars; if thirty
19 thousand dollars and under fifty thousand dollars, two hundred and
20 eight dollars; and if over fifty thousand dollars, ten dollars for
21 every ten thousand dollars excess over the said sum of fifty thousand
22 dollars.

Merchant's permission to sell ardent spirits.

28. And in every case in which the license to a merchant or

2 mercantile firm includes permission to sell wine, ardent spirits or a

3 mixture thereof, porter, ale or beer, by wholesale and retail, or by

4 retail only, if such merchant or firm (commencing business for the

5 first time) sell by wholesale and retail, an additional tax of one

6 hundred dollars; and if by retail only, forty dollars; and if such

7 license be to a merchant or mercantile firm to continue the privilege

8 of selling wine, ardent spirits or a mixture thereof, porter, ale or

9 beer, if by wholesale, or by wholesale and retail, or by retail only,

10 the tax shall be one per centum on the amount of such sales for the

11 year next preceding the time of obtaining said license, in addition to

12 the specific tax imposed on beginners; but said sales shall not be

13 estimated in ascertaining the amount of a merchant's license.

Merchant tailors and others.

29. Merchant tailors, lumber merchants, dealers in coal, ice or

2 wood, shall obtain licenses as merchants, and be assessed and taxed

3 thereon as other merchants are by the preceding sections of this act,

4 and shall be subject to like penalties for conducting such business

5 without a merchant's license.

Commission merchants.

30. The tax on every license to a commission merchant, for-

2 warding merchant, tobacco auctioneer or ship broker, shall be forty

3 dollars each if commencing business; and if to continue such busi-

4 ness after the same has been carried on for a year, the tax on such

5 license shall be two per centum on the amount of commissions re-

6 ceived; and this tax shall be in addition to such tax as may be

7 imposed on a license to such merchant or firm, to sell any goods,

8 wares or merchandise. All goods consigned to any such commission

9 merchant, forwarding merchant or tobacco auctioneer, whether such

10 goods be agricultural productions, or other articles exempted in the

11 hands of the producer or owner from taxation, shall be included as

12 subjects of taxation, under the provisions of this section.

Auctioneers.

31. On every license to an auctioneer or vendue master com-

2 mencing business, twenty-five dollars; and if the place of business

3 be in a town containing a population of three thousand inhabitants,

4 thirty-two dollars; if the population exceeds three thousand, an

5 additional tax of fifteen dollars for every thousand persons above

6 that number, and at that rate for any fractional excess less than one

7 thousand; but said specific tax shall in no case exceed three hun-

8 dred and fifty dollars. On every license to an auctioneer who deals

9 exclusively in real estate, two hundred and fifty dollars, and he shall

10 have the right to sell real estate at auction or otherwise. On every

11 license to an auctioneer or vendue master, in this section mentioned,

12 to continue the business after the same has been carried on for a

13 year, one-half of one per centum on the amount of taxable sales of

14 such auctioneer or vendue master; but in no case shall the tax on

15 such sales exceed one thousand dollars: provided, the tax to be paid

16 by auctioneers for the sales of molasses and sugar, shall in no case

17 exceed five hundred dollars for such sales; but the tax on sales of

18 other articles shall not be affected by this provision. But no sale

19 shall be made at any other place than the house named in the license

20 as the place of business, or at such other place as the person owning
21 the property is authorized to sell the same; and no goods shall be
22 consigned to such auctioneer for sale, unless the owner thereof has
23 obtained a merchant's license for a period as long as one whole year.

Common crier.

32. On every license to a common crier, if in a town of more
2 than 1,000 inhabitants, ten dollars; but he shall not be authorized
3 to act as such in the sale of any property belonging to any person,
4 unless such owner is authorized to sell such property without a
5 license, or has obtained a license to do so.

Sample merchants.

33. On every license to sell goods by sample, card or other rep-
2 resentation, two hundred dollars.

Express companies.

34. On every license permitting an express company to operate
2 throughout the state, fifty dollars.

Patent rights.

35. On every license to sell or barter the right to manufacture
2 or use any machinery or other thing patented to any person or com-
3 pany, under the laws of the United States, ten dollars in each
4 county; and no merchant shall sell the same without an additional
5 license.

Quack medicines.

36. On every license to sell patent, specific or quack medicines,
2 if by retail, twenty-five dollars, and if by wholesale, fifty dollars.

3 A person having a merchant's license may sell any such medicines
4 without any additional license, unless the same be sold on commis-
5 sion; in which case the additional license and tax shall be imposed.

Book agents.

37. On every license to a person obtaining subscriptions to books,
2 maps, prints, pamphlets or periodicals, twenty-five dollars for each
3 county. On every license to sell or in any manner furnish the same,
4 twenty-five dollars; if the person obtaining such license has not
5 been a resident of the state two years, the tax shall in each case be
6 two hundred dollars. But any person who has been a resident of
7 the state for two years, desiring to distribute or sell any religious
8 books, newspapers or pamphlets, may apply to the county or corpo-
9 ration court of each county in which he may desire to distribute or
10 sell the same; and such court, upon being satisfied that such person
11 is a proper person for such duty, may grant him a license, without
12 the imposition of any tax for the privilege.

Agents for renting houses and hiring negroes.

38. On every license to a person engaged as agent for the rent-
2 ing of houses, twenty-five dollars.

39. On every license to a person engaged as agent for the hiring
2 of negroes, fifty dollars.

Stallions.

40. On every license to the owner of a jackass or stallion, for
2 services of which the compensation is received, twice the amount of
3 such compensation, when the charge is for such service by the sea-

3

4 son ; and where such services are for less than a season, then twice

5 what a commissioner may judge to be a reasonable charge therefor.

6 The tax, however, in no case to be less than ten dollars.

Theatrical performances.

41. On every license permitting theatrical performances in a

2 public theatre or elsewhere, six dollars each week of such perform-

3 ances, notwithstanding the owner of the place of exhibition shall

4 have paid the license tax required on such theatre or rooms fitted

5 for public exhibitions.

42. On every license permitting the sale of refreshments in a

2 theatre during such performances, one hundred dollars for each

3 place of sale ; and no abatement shall be made, if the privilege be

4 exercised for a period of less than one year.

43. On every license permitting the proprietor or occupier of

2 any public theatre or room fitted for public exhibitions, to use the

3 same for such purposes for a year, twenty dollars, if such room be

4 in a town of less than five thousand inhabitants; forty dollars, if in

5 a town of more than five thousand and less than ten thousand inhabi-

6 tants, and sixty dollars in all other towns; but the land and house

7 in which such public shows are authorized, shall not be exempt from

8 taxation as other similar property.

44. On every license permitting any public show, exhibition or

2 performance, if in a corporate town, or within five miles thereof, for

3 each time of performance, ten dollars; if elsewhere, five dollars;

4 and for every exhibition of a circus, if within a corporate town, or

5 within five miles thereof, forty dollars; if elsewhere, twenty dol-
6 lars; and for every exhibition of a menagerie, if within a corporate
7 town, or five miles thereof, forty dollars; if elsewhere, twenty dol-
8 lars.   All such shows, exhibitions and performances, whether under
9 the same canvas or not, shall be construed to require separate
10 licenses therefor, whether exhibited for compensation or not; and
11 upon any such shows, exhibitions and performances being concluded,
12 so that an additional fee for admission be charged, in lieu of a return
13 check authorizing the holder to re-enter without charge, shall be
14 construed to require an additional license therefor.

Porter, ale and beer.

45. On every license to manufacture porter, ale and beer, or
2 cither, fifty dollars.   On every license to sell, by retail, porter, ale
3 or beer, twenty dollars; and if the business be continued for more
4 than one year, an additional tax of one per centum on the amount
5 of sales of the previous year.   But if the license be to retail to be
6 drank where sold, it shall be granted upon the certificate of the
7 county or corporation court, at the same terms and in every respect
8 as certificates are granted to ordinary keepers and merchants to
9 retail ardent spirits.

Stock brokers.

46. On every license to a broker who deals exclusively in stocks,
2 five hundred dollars; and he shall thereupon have the right to sell
3 the said stocks at auction or otherwise.

Bank note brokers.

47. On every license to a broker, five hundred dollars; if located
2 in a city with a population exceeding fifteen thousand of white popu-
3 lation, seven hundred and fifty dollars.

Insurance companies.

48. On every license to an agent or sub-agent of any insurance
2 company not chartered by this state, twenty-five dollars in each
3 county or city in which an office or place of business is situated;
4 and in addition thereto, a tax of one-half of one per cent. on the
5 whole amount of premiums received and assessments collected by
6 such agent or sub-agent or company within the state, as prescribed
7 by law.

Physicians and others.

49. On every license to a physician, surgeon or dentist, five
2 dollars each; and on every license to an attorney at law, five dol-
3 lars. If the yearly income derived from the practice of any such
4 callings or professions during the year next preceding the time of
5 obtaining such license shall exceed four hundred dollars, there shall
6 be an additional tax on the excess of one per centum; and this in-
7 come shall be included in the license tax.

Daguerreian artists.

50. On every license to the owner of a daguerreian or such like
2 gallery, by whatsoever name it may be known or called, if in a city
3 or incorporated town of less than five thousand inhabitants, twenty
4 dollars; if more than five thousand inhabitants, forty dollars; if

5 elsewhere, ten dollars; and if the yearly income derived from the
6 practice of said art exceed five hundred dollars in any county, city
7 or town, an additional tax of two per centum on such excess for the
8 year next preceding the time of obtaining such license: and such tax
9 shall be imposed whether an artist perform in a gallery or not.

Horses, mules, asses and jennets.

51. On every license to sell horses, mules, asses and jennets, which
2 are brought into this state for sale, ten dollars in each county; and
3 the act making general regulations concerning licenses shall be so
4 far modified that the certificate for obtaining such licenses may de-
5 signate the county or corporation as the place of sale. But the sale
6 of any other thing except specially authorized to be sold elsewhere,
7 shall name the particular place in the county or town whereat the
8 sale may be made, and horses so brought into this state, as often as
8 they are sold and the principal object of the sale is for profit, al-
9 though previously sold in this state, shall subject the person so
10 selling to the tax hereby imposed.

Horses, mules, &c. sold for profit.

52. On every license to sell for others, on commission or for
2 profit, horses, mules, asses, jennets, cattle, sheep and hogs, or either
3 of them, ten dollars in each county; and the sale may be made under
4 such license at any place in such county or corporation.

Carriages, buggies and other vehicles.

53. On every license to sell carriages, buggies, barouches, gigs,
2 wagons, and such like vehicles, manufactured out of this state, fifty
3 dollars.

Slaves bought for profit.

54. On every license to buy slaves on commission or for profit,
2 ten dollars in each county; and on the yearly income of such busi-
3 ness in all the counties (to be taxed but once), an additional tax of
4 two per centum on such income.

General provisions.

55. This act shall be construed to impose a tax on all occupa-
2 tions prohibited, unless the party exercising any thing so prohibited
3 show by his affidavit that his case comes under some of the excep-
4 tions to this act, or to the 38th chapter of the Code (edition 1860),
5 making general regulations concerning licenses.

56. No license shall be construed to grant any privilege beyond
2 the county or corporation wherein it is granted, unless it be ex-
3 pressly authorized.

57. Every license granting authority to sell, unless the license
2 be specially authorized by law for a county or corporation, shall be
3 at some specified house or place within such county or corporation.

58. Commissioners of the revenue shall furnish or cause to be
2 furnished to every tax payer to be found within his county, the forms
3 prescribed by the 65th section of chapter 35 of the Code.   He shall
4 require answers, according to said section, and with his books, shall
5 transmit said forms to the auditor of public accounts.

59. Any person continuing business, after any license obtained
2 by him shall have expired, without obtaining, on or before the day
3 his former license so expired, a license for the succeeding term, such

4 person shall be assessed with twice the amount of tax otherwise im-
5 posed on such license.

60. If a commissioner shall, in his list of licenses to be furnished
2 to the auditor of public accounts, charge or extend in any case a tax
3 less than the law requires, the auditor of public accounts shall de-
4 duct the amount omitted to be charged or extended, from the com-
5 pensation of the commissioner; and to enable the auditor to make
6 an examination of such lists, the commissioner shall return to him,
7 with his return of licenses, all interrogatories which may have been
8 propounded by him, under the direction of the auditor of public
9 accounts, and answered.

61. Any subject of taxation required to be listed under the pro-
2 visions of the 35th and 38th chapters of the Code, and not specially
3 taxed herein, shall be taxed as similar subjects.

62. After the year 1861 the auditor, in prescribing the form for
2 the commissioner's land book, shall so reform the 40th section of
3 chapter 35 of the Code, 2d edition, as to show in one column the
4 value of lands, exclusive of buildings, which value shall not be
5 changed.

63. The third chapter of the act, entitled an act imposing taxes
2 for the support of government, passed March 31st, 1860, be and the
3 same is hereby repealed.

64. This act shall be in force from its passage.

BILL No. 202.

SENATE BILL.

———

A BILL

Making appropriations for deficiencies in former appropriations, and
for defraying expenses of the General Assembly and Convention
now in session.

1. Be it enacted by the General Assembly, That the public
2 taxes and arrears of taxes due prior to the first day of October
3 1861, and not otherwise appropriated, and of all other branches of
4 revenue, and all public moneys, whether borrowed or not, not other-
5 wise appropriated by law, which shall come into the treasury prior
6 to the said first day of October 1861, shall constitute a general
7 fund, and in addition to the appropriations by the act passed the
8 17th March 1860, be appropriated for the fiscal year to close on the
9 30th day of September 1861, as follows, to wit:

10   To pay expenses of the general assembly for the session com-
11 mencing on the 7th day of January 1861, $125,000.

12   To each of the pages of the Senate and House of Delegates,
13 the sum of two dollars per day for each day of service as such; to
14 be paid upon the certificate of the clerk of the Senate and clerk of
15 the House of Delegates, respectively.

16   To Alfred Thornton, a porter to the Senate, for his services as
17 such, and also for his attention to the Senate chamber, clerk's office
18 and committee rooms of the Senate, and making fires in the same,
19 $2 50 per day; to be paid upon the certificate of the clerk of the
20 Senate.

21   To Richard Matthews, keeper of the keys of the capitol, for
22 his extra services during the last session, $1 for each night session
23 held.

24   To the further expenses of making fires and superintending
25 furnaces in the capitol, the customary allowances to the several per-
26 sons entitled to the same; to be paid upon the certificate of the
27 Superintendent of Public Buildings.

28   To pay the expenses of the convention to assemble on the 13th
29 February, 1861.

30   To pay expenses of commissioners to the city of Washington
31 and to the Southern States, eight dollars per day, and 20 cents per
32 mile to each commissioner.

33   For payment of so much of the interest on the public debt and
34 the gradual redemption thereof, and for investment omitted in the
35 last appropriation, $156,897.

36   For deficiency of interest due to the Literary fund, $1,000.

37   For deficiency in appropriation to pay expenses in comparing
38 polls in sundry elections, $ 350.

39   For deficiency in appropriation to pay the salaries of judges and
40 other officers, $1,000.

41   For deficiency in appropriation to pay for slaves sentenced for
42 crime, $10,000.

43   For deficiency in supplies for the support of convicts and trans-
44 ports, $3,000.

45   For deficiency in appropriation to pay for brigade inspectors,
46 adjutants, clerks, musicians, &c. $30,000.

47   For deficiency in appropriation to pay the salary of the adjutant
48 general, $500.

49   For deficiency in appropriation for expenses of visitors to the
50 Virginia military institute, $2,200.

51   For deficiency in the Military contingent fund, $1,800.

52   To pay for the publication of defaulting officers, $200.

53   For deficiency in appropriation for the annual support of Vir-
54 ginia military institute, $5,790.

55   For deficiency in appropriation to pay for rations, clothing, &c.,
56 of the public guard and the interior guard at the penitentiary,
57 $5,000.

58   For deficiency in appropriation to pay for collecting and distri-
59 buting arms, $1,800.

60   For deficiency in appropriation for taking lists of taxable pro-
61 perty, $5,000.

62   For deficiency in appropriation to the Western lunatic asylum,
63 $500.

64   For deficiency in appropriation heretofore made to and uncalled
65 for by the Eastern lunatic asylum, $31,250.

4 Bill No. 202.

66   For construction of the Trans-Alleghany lunatic asylum, addi-
67 tional to that heretofore appropriated, $50,000.

68   For deficiency in appropriation to pay expenses of lunatics con-
69 fined in county jails, $1,800.

70   For deficiency to pay expenses of civil suits, $1,000.

71   For deficiency in appropriation for the repairs of the governor's
72 house and furnishing the same with fuel and lights, $3,700.

73   For deficiency in appropriation for the repairs of the capitol,
74 $4,500.

75   For deficiency in appropriation for publishing Grattan's Reports,
76 $3,618.

77   For reprinting 500 copies of the 5th volume of Leigh's Reports,
78 $1,250.

79   For 4,500 copies of Mayo's Guide, $11,250.

80   For printing to be done in pursuance of the act of the 20th
81 February 1858, and for books for public offices, $16,000.

82   For 10,000 copies of the second edition of the Code, $20,000.

83   To the Secretary of the Commonwealth, for preparing the second
84 edition of the Code, $2,000.

85   For completing the statue of Nelson, $4,500.

86   For erecting the statue of Nelson and allegorical figures on
87 Washington monument, $23,400.

88   For balance of appropriation of act of 21st February 1854, for
89 Galt's statue of Jefferson, $4,000.

90   For permanently enclosing the birth place of Washington and

91 the home and graves of his progenitors in America, and marking
92 the same by suitable tablets, under act of the 20th January, 1858,
93 $4,860 79.

94   For balance of money appropriated for enlargement of medical
95 college, under act of March 1st, 1860, $15,000.

96   For the per diem and milage of electors of president and vice-
97 president and pay of secretary to the college of electors, $1,200;
98 and to William Teller, page of the electoral college, $25.

99   For commissions to sheriffs remaining unpaid, and to be paid
100 upon the warrant of the auditor of public accounts, $1,500.

101   For deficiency in appropriations to pay commissioners for list-
102 ing free negroes, $120.

103   To meet claims allowed and outstanding for expenses growing
104 out of the John Brown raid, $906 61.

105   To George W. Munford, J. M. Bennett and Wm. H. Richard-
106 son, for auditing the claims for the defence of Harpers Ferry and
107 the execution of John Brown, each $500.

108   For rewards under act of 17th March 1856, and claims under
109 the 45th chapter of the Code, $5,000.

2. In case any of the appropriations herein made, are in whole
2 or in part included in any general or special appropriation act,
3 heretofore passed, no more money shall be paid under this act than
4 such sum or sums which remain unpaid under such acts.

3. So much of the public revenue as may be received into the
2 public treasury after the 30th day of September 1861, and the sur-

3 plus of all other appropriations made prior to that date, unexpended
4 within the two fiscal years, ending respectively on the 30th of Sep-
5 tember 1860, and 30th of September 1861, and all moneys not
6 otherwise appropriated by law, shall constitute a general fund, to
7 defray such expenses authorized by law as are not herein particu-
8 larly provided for, and to defray the usual allowances for support
9 and transportation to lunatic asylums and other current expenses of
10 the commonwealth, in the fiscal year which will commence on the
11 first day of October 1861, and terminate on the 30th September
12 1862. And the auditor of public accounts is hereby authorized and
13 required to issue his warrants in the same manner as if the same
14 had been specifically mentioned, subject to such exceptions, limita-
15 tions and conditions as the general assembly have prescribed, or
16 may deem it proper to annex and prescribe by law: provided, that
17 nothing in this act contained shall be so construed as to authorize
18 the auditor of public accounts to issue his warrant or warrants in
19 satisfaction of any judgment or decree of any court of law or equity
20 against the commonwealth, for a sum of or over three hundred dol-
21 lars, without a special appropriation by law.

4. The payments to the military institute, for support, to the
2 lunatic asylums, for support and transportation of patients, and to
3 the institution for the education of the deaf and dumb and the blind
4 shall be made, one-fourth in advance on the first day of October,
5 one-half on the first day of January (if the visitors or directors so
6 require), and the remaining one-fourth on the first day of April.

5. This act shall be in force from its passage.

BILL No. 213.

SENATE BILL.

A BILL

To authorize the appointments of Inspectors of Leather.

1. Be it enacted by the General Assembly, That the Governor
2 is hereby authorized to appoint an inspector of leather for the
3 several counties and towns in which it may be necessary.

2. This act shall be in force from its passage.

P 158
cr 2 2 8 7 4

SENATE BILL.

A BILL

In relation to printing the Acts of Assembly.

1. Be it enacted by the General Assembly, That hereafter it
2. shall be the duty of the public printer to cause the Acts of Assem-
3. bly of Virginia to be printed with type, paper and style conforming
4. to that of the volume containing the Acts of the session of 1857–8.

2. This act shall be in force from its passage.

BILL No. 223.

D. 15 ?
CV. L 2?7-t

SENATE BILL.

———

A BILL

To amend the 6th section of an act for the relief of the Banks of this Commonwealth.

    1. Be it enacted by the General Assembly, That the 6th section

2 of the act passed on 28th day of February, 1861, entitled, "An act

3 for the relief of the Banks of this Commonwealth," be amended

4 and re-enacted so as to read as follows:

5   "§ 6. On the payment of every note, bill or draft, payable at the

6 cities of Baltimore, Philadelphia, New York and Boston, which may

7 be hereafter discounted by any bank or branch during the suspen-

8 sion of specie payment by it, such bank or branch shall pay to the

9 party for whom such paper was discounted, the excess of exchange

10 at the time of such payment over and above the rate between the

11 point where such bank or branch is located and the point where

12 such paper is payable, at the time such bank or branch suspended

13 specie payment; and on failure of such bank or branch to pay such

14 excess on paper hereafter discounted, the party entitled thereto may

15 recover the same by warrant before any justice of the peace, or

16 when the amount is over fifty dollars, by motion on ten days' notice

17 before any court of the county or corporation where such bank or

18 branch is located."

2. This act shall be in force from its passage.

BILL No. 225.

SENATE BILL.

A BILL

To authorize the Treasurer of the State to destroy certain bank notes now in his office, and such as may be received in future.

1. Be it enacted by the General Assembly, That the Treasurer
2 of the Commonwealth be authorized and required to destroy the
3 bank notes now on deposit in his office, which have been returned
4 to said office for cancellation or renewal by the several banks of the
5 State; and in future all such bank notes so returned to said office,
6 after the same shall have been cancelled or renewed, shall be de-
7 stroyed by the said Treasurer and the agent of such bank so return-
8 ing their notes.

2. This act shall commence and be in force from its passage.

BILL No. 229.

D. 161
C. 2287-691

SENATE BILL.

A BILL

To amend the fifteenth section of chapter 109 of the Code of Virginia,
(second edition.)

I. Be it enacted by the General Assembly, That the fifteenth
2 section of chapter one hundred and nine of the second edition of
3 the Code of Virginia, be amended and re-enacted so as to read as
4 follows :

5   "§ 15. When a decree for a separation forever, or for a limited
6 period, shall have been pronounced in a suit for a divorce from bed
7 and board, it may be revoked at any time thereafter by the same
8 court by which it was pronounced, under such regulations and re-
9 strictions as the court may impose upon the joint application of the
10 parties ; and upon their producing satisfactory evidence of their
11 reconciliation, and when a divorce from bed and board has been
12 decreed for abandonment or desertion, and five years shall have
13 elapsed from the abandonment or desertion without such reconcilia-
14 tion, the court may, upon the application of the injured party and
15 the production of satisfactory evidence, whether taken theretofore,
16 or in support of such application, decree or divorce from the bond

17 of matrimony: provided, the court shall be of opinion that such
18 decree would have been proper, when the decree from bed and
19 board was pronounced, had five years then elapsed, and the whole
20 evidence adduced upon said application been before the court, and
21 that no reconciliation is probable.

  3. This act shall be in force from its passage.

BILL No. 230.

SENATE BILL.

A BILL

To amend the forty-fifth section of chapter 171 of the Code of Virginia.

1. Be it enacted by the General Assembly, That the forty-fifth

2 section of chapter one hundred and seventy-one of the Code, be

3 amended and re-enacted so as to read as follows:

4   "§ 45. If a defendant against whom judgment is entered in the

5 office, shall, before it becomes final, appear and plead to issue, it

6 shall be set aside, unless an order for enquiry of damages has been

7 executed; in which case it shall not be set aside without good cause.

8 And in no case shall the judgment so entered in the office be set

9 aside, unless the plea be verified by affidavit or good cause be shown

10 for the failure so to verify it. Any such issue may be tried at the

11 same term, unless the defendant show good cause for a continuance."

SENATE BILL.

A BILL

Authorizing the Petersburg railroad company to increase its capital stock.

1. Be it enacted, That it shall be lawful for the stockholders of
2 the Petersburg railroad company, in general meeting, to increase
3 the capital stock of said company by directing the issue of new
4 stock to the holders of the present stock, to such an amount as the
5 said stockholders, in general meeting, may think fit: provided, the
6 amount of new stock so to be issued, shall not exceed one-half the
7 amount of the present stock of said company.

2. The said company, if the stockholders shall so direct, shall
2 be authorized to issue certificates of stock for half shares or other
3 fractions of shares.

3. This act shall be in force from its passage.

SENATE BILL.

A BILL

To amend the charter of Brown's Gap turnpike company.

1. Be it enacted by the General Assembly, That the second
2 section of the act passed March —, 1853, entitled, "An act incor-
3 porating the Brown's Gap turnpike company," be amended and
4 re-enacted so as to read as follows :

5 "§ 2. When one hundred shares of said capital stock shall have
6 been subscribed, the subscribers or their personal representives shall
7 be, and are hereby incorporated by the name of the "Brown's Gap
8 turnpike company," with power to construct their road not less than
9 18 feet in width, and of a grade not exceeding four degrees at any
10 point, with authority to demand and receive of all who use not less
11 than one mile of said road, tolls for the use of the same, and the
12 said company shall be subject to the provisions of the Code of Vir-
13 ginia on the subject of turnpike companies, except so far as the
14 same shall be in conflict with the provisions of this act.

15 The county court of Albemarle is authorized to transfer such
16 sections and portions of the county road, now used in connection
17 with the road of said company, upon such terms as may be agreed

18 upon between them, to be incorporated into the road of said com-
19 pany : provided, the same be first recommended by a report of one
20 or more of the road commissioners of said county, all the justices
21 of the county having been first duly summoned to consider the
22 same, and a majority of those present concurring therein."

   2. This act shall be in force from its passage.

SENATE BILL.

A BILL

To incorporate a company to construct a railroad from Strasburg to Winchester.

1. Be it enacted by the General Assembly, That it shall be
2 lawful to open books at Strasburg, in the county of Shenandoah,
3 upon ten days' notice, under the direction of J. C. Richardson, John
4 F. Balthis, Edward Zea, John Pirkey, P. F. Everly, John S. Hupp,
5 or any three of them, at such time or times as they may deem
6 proper, and in such other place or places and under the direction
7 of such agents as the commissioners acting may appoint, for the
8 purpose of receiving subscriptions to the amount of four hundred
9 thousand dollars, divided into shares of fifty dollars each, to consti-
10 tute a joint capital stock, for the purpose of constructing a railroad
11 from Strasburg to Winchester, to be connected with the Manassas
12 Gap railroad at Strasburg, and with the Alexandria, Loudoun and
13 Hampshire railroad at Winchester.

2. Whenever one hundred thousand dollars of the stock shall be
2 subscribed, the subscribers and their successors shall be and are
3 hereby incorporated into a company, by the name of the " Strasburg

4 railroad company;" subject to all the provisions and entitled to all

5 the benefits and powers conferred by the provisions of chapters

6 fifty-six and fifty-seven of the Code of Virginia, so far as the same

7 may be applicable and not inconsistent with the provisions of this

8 charter.

    3. This act shall commence and be in force from its passage.

SENATE BILL.

A BILL

Transferring the Cacapon and North Branch turnpike to the county court of Hampshire county.

Whereas, it is represented to the General Assembly of the State
2 of Virginia, that the travel upon the road known as the Cacapon
3 and North Branch turnpike, in the county of Hampshire, is insuffi-
4 cient to furnish the amount of toll necessary to keep the road in
5 proper repair; therefore,

1. Be it enacted by the General Assembly, That the turnpike
2 known as the Cacapon and North Branch turnpike in the county of
3 Hampshire, be and the same is hereby transferred to and vested in
4 the county court of Hampshire, to be held and kept in repair for
5 public use, and to be in all respects subject to the authority of said
6 court as other public roads in said county: provided, however, that
7 the assent to the transfer shall first be obtained of such stockholders,
8 other than the State, as may assemble in general meeting, after pub-
9 lication of notice of the time and place for such meeting, for two
10 months.

2. This act shall be in force from its passage.

A BILL

To prevent the suspension of work on the Covington and Ohio railroad.

Whereas, the contractors on the Covington and Ohio railroad
2 are sustaining great loss in consequence of the depreciation of State
3 stock, mainly caused by the political troubles of the country, and
4 will be compelled to abandon their contracts unless some relief is
5 granted: and whereas, great loss would be sustained by the State if
6 the work on the Covington and Ohio railroad should be suspended;
7 therefore,

1. Be it enacted by the General Assembly, That the Board of
2 Public Works be, and they are hereby authorized to increase, to a
3 rate not exceeding ten per.cent., the prices which have been con-
4 tracted to be paid to the contractors on the Covington and Ohio
5 railroad: provided, that such increase of prices shall only be allowed
6 to the contractors who are now actually engaged in the construction
7 of said road: and provided, further, that such increase of prices
8 shall only continue to the first day of January, 1862.

2. This act shall be in force from its passage.

BILL No. 239.

.

SENATE BILL.

A BILL

For compensating the families of persons killed by accidents.

Whereas, no action at law is now maintainable against a person
2 who, by his wrongful act, neglect or default, may have caused the
3 death of another person, and it is right and expedient that the
4 wrongdoer in such case should be answerable in damages for the
5 injury so caused by him:

1. Be it therefore enacted by the General Assembly, That when-
2 soever the death of a person shall be caused by wrongful act, neglect
3 or default, and the act, neglect or default is such as would (if death
4 had not ensued) have entitled the party injured to maintain an action
5 and recover damages in respect thereof, then and in every such case
6 the person who would have been liable, if death had not ensued,
7 shall be liable to an action for damages, notwithstanding the death
8 of the person injured.

2. And be it enacted, That every such action shall be for the
2 benefit of the wife, husband, parent and child of the person whose
3 death shall have been so caused, and shall be brought by and in the
4 name of the personal representative of the person deceased; and in

5 every such action, the jury may give such damages as they may

6 think proportioned to the injury resulting from such death, to the

7 parties respectively for whom and for whose benefit such action shall

8 be brought; and the amount so recovered, after deducting the costs

9 not recovered from the defendant or defendants, shall be divided

10 amongst the before-mentioned parties in such shares as the jury by

11 their verdict shall find and direct: provided, always, that not more

12 than one action shall lie for and in respect of the same subject mat-

13 ter of complaint, and that every such action shall be commenced

14 within twelve calendar months after the death of such deceased

15 person.

    3. And be it enacted, That the following words and expressions

2 are intended to have the meanings hereby assigned to them respec-

3 tively, that is to say: the word "parent" shall include father

4 and mother and grandfather and grandmother, and step-father and

5 step-mother; and the word " child " shall include son and daughter

6 and grandson and grand daughter, and step-son and step-daughter.

    4. And be it enacted, That this act shall be taken and construed

2 to be remedial only, and not in derogation of the common law, and

3 shall come into operation from and immediately after the passing

4 thereof.

SENATE BILL.

A BILL

Authorizing the amendment of the charter of the Holliday's cove railroad company.

1. Be it enacted by the General Assembly, That the council of
2   the city of Wheeling is hereby authorized, at its discretion, and for
3   such consideration (the payment whereof shall be properly secured)
4   as may be agreed on between it and the Holliday's cove railroad
5   company, to relieve the said company from the restrictions contained
6   in sections 7, 8, 9, 10 and 11 of an act passed March 30th, 1860,
7   entitled, "An act to incorporate the Holliday's cove railroad com-
8   pany: such release to be acknowledged and recorded in the clerk's
9   office of the county court of Ohio county.

2. This act shall be in force from its passage.

SENATE BILL.

A BILL

Establishing a Board of Claims.

1. Be it enacted by the General Assembly, That the Auditor of
2 Public Accounts, the Second Auditor and the Registrar of the Land
3 Office be, and they are hereby constituted a "Board of Claims," to
4 examine and allow all claims upon the Commonwealth which are
5 legally or equitably chargeable thereto, and which cannot be paid
6 by the Auditor of Public Accounts under existing laws. Any per-
7 son desiring to have any such claim audited and paid, may, within
8 five years after the claim originated and became payable, file with
9 the said board a declaration in writing, verified by affidavit, setting
10 forth the facts upon which he claims relief; and the said board
11 shall grant such relief as, upon the facts properly proved, shall
12 appear just and equitable. The board shall in no case pay a claim
13 exceeding in amount one hundred dollars; which payment shall be
14 upon the warrant of the Auditor of Public Accounts, founded upon
15 the award of the said board. Claims exceeding one hundred dollars
16 may be examined, and their payment recommended to the General

17 Assembly. The said board shall file all their awards and recom-
18 mendations with the Auditor of Public Accounts, who shall, in his
19 official report to the General Assembly, make an accurate statement
20 of all cases upon which such board may have acted, and the grounds
21 upon which the said board may may have granted or refused relief.

    2. This act shall be in force from its passage.

SENATE BILL.

A BILL

Offering for sale a portion of the armory grounds.

1. Be it enacted by the General Assembly, That the superinten-
2 dent of the armory shall cause to be marked off so much of the
3 armory grounds as may, in the opinion of the Governor and himself,
4 be spared without impairing the efficiency of the armory, as a place
5 .for the manufacture of arms as contemplated by law, and cause
6 accurate maps thereof to be made, and shall advertise such surplus
7 ground for sale, by inviting written proposals for the same up to the
8 first day of December, 1861, and shall report a list of all such pro-
9 posals to the Governor, to be by him submitted to the next General
10 Assembly for its ratification or rejection.

BILL No. 254.

A BILL

To provide quarters for the Public Guard, and a depot for arms and munitions of war at the city of Richmond.

1. Be it enacted by the General Assembly, That the Governor
2 shall cause to be prepared suitable designs and plans for the build-
3 ings necessary for quarters for the Public Guard, and a depot for
4 arms and munitions of war, and cause the same to be erected on a
5 site to be selected and purchased by him and the superintendent of
6 the armory for that purpose.

2. Be it further enacted, That the sum of   thousand dollars
2 is hereby appropriated for the purposes aforesaid, out of any money
3 in the treasury not otherwise appropriated.

SENATE BILL.

A BILL

To authorize the Alexandria, Loudoun and Hampshire Railroad Company to increase its capital stock, and to receive payment in land.

1. Be it enacted by the General Assembly, That the directors
2 of the Alexandria, Loudoun and Hampshire Railroad company may,
3 from time to time, increase their capital stock by new subscriptions,
4 any may receive payment for shares of said company, at such rates
5 as may be agreed upon between them and the subscribers, any lands
6 situated in this State and State of Maryland in the county of
7 Alleghany: provided, the said company shall, within ten years
8 after their railroad shall have been completed to Piedmont in
9 Hampshire, make a bona fide sale and transfer of all the lands thus
10 received in payment for such subscriptions.

www.ingramcontent.com/pod-product-compliance
Lightning Source LLC
Chambersburg PA
CBHW021115270326
41929CB00009B/888